TOWARDS
A LIBERATING PEACE

TOWARDS A LIBERATING PEACE

✻

Rajni Kothari, Richard Falk,
Mary Kaldor, Lim Teck Ghee,
Giri Deshingkar, Jimoh Omo-Fadaka,
Tamas Szentes, José A. Silva Michelena,
Ismael Sabri-Abdalla, Yoshikazu Sakamoto

✻ ✻ ✻

THE UNITED NATIONS UNIVERSITY
Tokyo

NEW HORIZONS PRESS
New York

LOKVANI
New Delhi

TOWARDS A LIBERATING PEACE

Published in 1988 by:
New Horizons Press
777, United Nations Plaza, New York 10017
Tel: (212)972-9877, Cable: COUNINTERP NEW YORK

in association with
Lokvani
a division of The Foundation for Humane Values
A-36, Chittaranjan Park, New Delhi - 110019, India
Tel: 6410206

and

The United Nations University
Toho Seimei Building, 15-1 Shibuya 2-chome, Shibuya-ku
Tokyo 150, Japan
Tel: (03)499-2811 Telex: J25442 Cable: UNATUNIV TOKYO

Copyright © The United Nations University, 1988

All rights reserved

ISBN 0-945257-06-6 Hb
ISBN 0-945257-00-7 Pb

Typeset by Computype (a division of Third World Publications Pvt. Ltd.)
61, Madhuvan, Shakarpur, Delhi 110 092
Printed by Smitu Kothari and Kunal Mullick
at Impress Offset, NOIDA, U. P.

PRINTED IN INDIA

This book is dedicated to the memory of
José Augustine Michelena
Member of the Core Group of the United Nations University Project on Peace And Global Transformation of which this book is the first composite outcome and in the making of which, as well as to the project as a whole, he had made a substantial contribution.

The United Nations University's Programme on Peace and Global Transformation was a major world-wide project whose purpose was to develop new insights about the interlinkages between questions of peace, conflict resolution, and the process of transformation. The research in this project, under six major themes, was co-ordinated by a 10-member core group in different regions of the world: East Asia, South-East Asia(including the Pacific), South Asia, the Arab region, Africa, Western Europe, Eastern Europe, North America, and Latin America. The themes covered were: Conflicts over Natural Resources; Security, Vulnerability, and Violence; Human Rights and Cultural Survival in a Changing Pluralistic World; The Role of Science and Technology in Peace and Transformation; and Global Economic Crisis. The project also included a study on Peace and Regional Security as part of the U.N. Year of Peace.

Contents

Preface i

Introduction 1

Militarisation: The Imaginary War 21

The World Economic Crisis 50

Conflicts over Natural Resources 88

Human Rights, Political Democracy and the Survival of Cultures 123

Conclusion: Transforming the State 147

Preface

We are living in a world where there is a widespread sense of general malaise, made worse by crises, new or emerging, of one kind or another at the local, regional and global levels. At one end of the spectrum, there is the constant threat of a cataclysmic nuclear war. At the other, even without a war, nuclear or conventional, hundreds of millions of people are facing slow death because of destitution, disease, forced migration, political and cultural repression and other denials of life-sustenance by the elites in authority.

The terror of instant annihilation remains unrelieved by the nature of political institutions, be they liberal, socialist, nationalist or of other persuasions. With the exception of a few States, e.g., Brazil, Argentina, and to some extent China, where the process of 'redemocratisation' is under way, an ever larger number of States are getting militarised; armed threat, repression and coercion are the currencies of power in many parts of the world today.

The rapid and rapacious destruction of life-sustaining natural resources goes on in tandem with the process of militarisation. Again, regardless of the nature of the State, human rights are being violated routinely in several countries. In the poor two-thirds of the world, even the right to life is flouted by many regimes. The struggle for sheer survival goes on simultaneously with the struggle against cultural destruction. To add to all this, the world is in the grip of an unprecedented economic crisis; no political or economic system has been able to extricate itself completely from it. The global economic crisis has manifested itself in conflicts between the 'North' and the 'South', the 'West' and the 'East', within regions and within countries. What is most frightening is the banality of the crises with which we live every day. We routinely accept their underlying causes and think about fragmented firefighting 'solutions' only to tide over some particularly aggravating symptoms.

It is abundantly clear that the existing global 'State-system' is incapable of managing international problems of war and economic management. It is equally clear that the State as an institution is also proving inadequate in resolving problems of intrasociety violence, economic distress—in a large number of cases, widespread destitution—ecological damage and cultural destruction. On the other hand, the people who would have been led to believe that the State would be their liberator and protector have lost control over the State and its institutions, including political parties. The peoples' struggles for survival, justice, dignity and cultural autonomy are fragmented, localised, situation-bound and therefore largely ineffective. When it comes to changing the larger system, whether national or global, past experiments in the seizure of State power by those who claimed to act on behalf of the dispossessed have often ended in reproducing different manifestations of the same problem.

The intellectual quest for diagnosis of the problem and its solutions has remained fragmented. Even if we forget about those academics and intellectuals who have been coopted by the State system and who lend their services for the management of the most threatening symptoms, and focus, instead, on concerned scholars and thinkers in different fields and regions, we find that even they tend to take a view too specialised to produce a holistic diagnosis and multi-faceted remedial action. Scholarly research has singularly failed to produce usable wisdom. On the other hand, those who come up with visions of desirable futures neglect to ensure a fit between the vision and the forces at work.

It is not as if alternative visions and follow-up strategies, both socio-political and intellectual, have not been tried. They have been tried so often. The October Revolution in the USSR, the various socialist revolutions in Eastern Europe, China, Vietnam and elsewhere, as well as the 'socialist' restructuring of liberal democratic

Preface

polities in Western Europe, represented major efforts in this direction. Equally major were the variety of efforts at building independent, self-reliant and democratic systems in the post-colonial world, and in countries such as Yugoslavia, a leader of the non-aligned world. Yet today, all of these face crises of one form or another and are deeply affected by the global malaise described above. And everywhere the processes of fragmentation and/or cooptation are becoming evident, though, no doubt, in almost all these regions there is some evidence of both social and intellectual restlessness.

The United Nations University (UNU) has joined the intellectual quest for a holistic diagnosis of the crisis and for remedial action by launching an action-oriented research programme entitled Peace and Global Transformation. The programme is based on the conviction that the issues of peace are inextricably related to the process of transformation; a stable and just peace is unattainable without realising a desirable transformation of the international political, military, economic and cultural order and similar transformations within States; on the other hand, the processes of transformation are difficult to pursue and remain unattainable in the absence of peace.

We, the contributors to this document, have constituted ourselves into a 'Core Group' to initiate, pursue, monitor and sum up the research activities of the Peace and Global Transformation programme throughout its five-year duration (1983-1987). This way, we believe, we can avoid the fragmentation of the research effort and knit it into a whole. This initial statement of ours on the *problematique* of peace and transformation describes our multidimensional approach and indicates the direction in which we believe the solutions lie. We hope to follow up this initial exercise with a more elaborate statement which will be informed by the theoretical and empirical research undertaken under the Peace and Global Transformation programme in various parts of the globe.

There are many groups these days sounding alarms and proposing solutions. We do not belittle such organised efforts to promote rationality and humanistic solutions through appeals to the leaders of governments round the world. We have in mind, particularly, the notable work of the Brandt and Palme Commissions, the Club of Rome, Restructuring International Order (RIO), the Bariloche Foundation and various United Nations agencies and commissions. Yet, we feel these initiatives, valuable as they are, are being treated as no more than pinpricks in the conscience of the rich and the powerful.

Our effort is directed toward informing and strengthening the constructive elements among those who are engaged already in struggles for change through various social movements at the 'grassroots' or harbour in their hearts and minds varying degrees of empathy for such struggles, even if their own institutional locations happen to be within the prevailing network of oppressive structures.

Our effort is also based on listening more than on telling. We believe that it is important to gather together the diversity of torments, the many cries of pain, in our world, as well as to report on those responses that seem hopeful in a variety of settings. We seek to approach the overall situation as many-sided in symptom and prescription. Yet we are also intent on discerning connections, pervasive themes and wide-ranging structures. In this respect our goal is both to present unity amid apparent diversity and diversity amid an evident unity.

We believe that the situation calls for plain language and non-technical forms of understanding. We hope to stimulate reflection, discussion and even controversy, but most of all, curative action. We see great opportunities to build bridges, to empower those who are weak and discouraged, and to build up the aspiring forces of society in their last-ditch encounter with authoritarianism and militarism that threaten not only life, but dignity and identity as the wellsprings of the human spirit.

This statement of ours is an outcome of contributions from all the 'Core Group' members. The Core Group as a whole discussed the draft and the Drafting Committee appointed by it (Rajni Kothari, Richard Falk, Mary Kaldor and Giri Deshingkar) was entrusted with the task of producing the final text. While all of us discussed the chapters and made suggestions about their content, style, organisation, etc., we cannot claim that each one of us agrees with every single detail or even all the conclusions in the final version.

Preface

(The responsibility for the contents of the final version rests with the Drafting Committee.) We come from different regions of the globe. Our vantage points, given our different ideological, disciplinary and cultural backgrounds, are necessarily different. We accept these differences, even celebrate them. Nevertheless, after working together, we have come to realise how much we share with each other.

For enabling us to come together and work together our collective and grateful thanks go to Dr. Soedjatmoko, the UNU Rector, who was the first to encourage us to translate the original Conceptual Paper into a concrete research programme and to Dr. Kinhide Mushakoji, Vice-Rector, whom we count as one of us in the 'Core'; the latter has, in many ways, worked harder than the rest of us for the P&GT Major Project. We also owe our thanks to Dr. Janusz Golebiowski, Senior Programme Officer, for serving as an intellectual critic as well as a nurturant administrator. And, of course, we gratefully record our thanks to the very large number of individuals in various regional 'networks' who were brought together for this programme, the large variety of persons at the Tokyo Centre, the Programme Office in Delhi and in our respective institutions in the various countries and regions without whose silent contribution this statement of ours would not have been possible.

Rajni Kothari
Richard Falk
Mary Kaldor
Lim Teck Ghee
Giri Deshingkar
Jimoh Omo-Fadaka
Tamas Szentes
Jose A. Silva Michelena
Ismael Sabri-Abdalla
Yoshikazu Sakamoto

1
Introduction

The character of the challenge we face today at the world level or indeed at any other level is elusive and controversial. It is impossible to isolate 'the problem' and say *this* is it! Confusion persists. It is difficult for the people of the world to envisage a line or lines of response.

In such a troubled setting neither established leaders nor traditional opposition leaders are able to define clearly, much less effect, a convincing resolution of the diverse challenges facing the organised political communities throughout the world. At the same time, the severity of problems leads to a variety of attempts to 'fix' the situation. In this atmosphere, coercion becomes an easy substitute for political imagination. Thus, across the globe, an orgy of militarism has ensued; repression of basic rights of the people is on the increase; resort to violence to maintain stability or to effect change is rampant. War and terrorism define the dialogue between those that have and those that want or are aggrieved.

But simultaneously with all this, our field of awareness has also enlarged to take in the mass ordeal of everyday existence for the poor of the world. We cannot escape the image of malnourished children by the millions facing a life of illness, probably with retarded faculties even if they are lucky enough to survive. We are appalled, as well, by the millions and millions of refugees who live more or less permanently in desolate camps, often treated harshly and inhumanly. We also cannot escape the obscenity of the luxury and waste that divert the elites of the world, with their estates and racing cars, their jewels and extravagant vacations, their total self-indulgence beneath the gaze of the sad-eyed poor and that of the growing hordes of persons displaced from their homelands. Only recently, we are also becoming aware that our generation on this planet, disturbed as it is by a series of deepening crises, may well be considered blessed compared to what our descendants in the next century may come to experience. It is now perfectly realistic to imagine a denatured landscape in which brute force prevails and the struggle for individual and class existence is continuous, or its seemingly opposite, a computerised mantle of totalitarian bureaucracy, a world devoid of feelings and humour. Lyrics of rock songs and popular films convey this message as a kind of cultural distress signal. It would be edifying to invite world leaders to offer their response to films like *Mad Max, Brazil, 1984, Aakrosh* and *Damul.*

Are we taking these ominous forebodings too seriously? Is it not still possible to believe in the resilience of nature and human life? Are we not already taking steps to alleviate the dangers, or at least those crises that confront us with the prospect of extinction? To be sure, there are responses that express an overall preference for preservation. Outbursts of violence and warfare still operate as 'exceptions' on the world scene as a whole; disaster relief mitigates, or appears to, the most acute suffering due to drought, earthquakes and floods. Confrontation between antagonistic forces gives way, after bloody interludes, to a variety of ceasefires. Generally, the most glaring excesses are contained, except at the local level where a variety of *pogroms* have ravaged particular peoples in country after country and where locales of 'natural disasters' are abandoned by the affluent; and only the poor, the aged and the most vulnerable are left behind to suffer.

Preventing the worst is not nearly enough. Tensions persist at intolerable levels. The worst has been tasted time and again, often irrevocably in the form of genocide. As a result, total irreversible collapse forms a vital part of our self-understanding as a species in this historic era. Humanity has a record of many failings in its short history but for the most part, human viability was threatened only from without—by an angry god at the end of his or her patience

Introduction

or by a divine plan to bring existence to a dramatic end, or by some arbitrary quirk of natural forces operating beyond the reach of human control. Because earlier threats to existence were external, it was always possible to shape social response, either by way of waiting for the end or through conversion of energy into a programme of positive action.

The new circumstance is different. Today, technology enables global reach and apocalyptic threat. To survive by threatening extinction, a prospect made vivid by the horrifying menace of nuclear winter, is what we mean by deterrence. To modernise by threatening culture is what we mean by development. To modernise through 'Star Wars' technologies is, at the outer limit, what we mean by security. Our moral sensibilities are torn asunder by such postures. Without respect for the innocence of others there can be no human identity. Without respect for the nurturing of nature there can be no sense of participation in the surroundings of human existence; even if affluent, we will wander the planet as aliens. Walking the streets of Hong Kong or Houston or Lagos or Calcutta conveys an impression that collapsed human beings are being scattered as litter; experienced as problems of garbage collection. More than a quarter million serious victims of poisonous gas and chemicals were left unattended, many months after the haunting catastrophe of Bhopal.

The same tragedy of neglect applies to the collapsing cultures of ethnic minorities in plural societies. Even in the so-called 'developed' world there is a breakdown of community·so profound that many turn to a life of drugs, alcohol and diverting entertainments to dull the anguish of wandering the planet as strangers obsessed by a meaningless craving for what is no longer clearly recollected, a search for a definite place amid an incoherent criss-cross of rights, duties, rituals and customs.

And so, desperate quests for identity and meaning are everywhere taking such diverse forms as to be often unrecognisable from one setting to the next. Affinities are often hidden. There are poor in the North, rich in the South. There are traditional islands of identity in the North, abandoned or relinquished traditions in the South. What we wish to underline is the painful experience almost everywhere that is associated with struggles to sustain individual and group identity or to achieve a meaningful life in its absence. The passions unleashed around the quest for identity have encouraged the growth and regeneration of new and old forms of fundamentalism and even of idolatories. These dogmas insist on the unconditional virtues and claims of a part of the larger community as against the rights and opposing claims of another part or even of the whole. When the aroused Shias of Iran terrorise their secular neighbours or put to death hapless Baha'is, we observe the demonic energies of fundamentalism at work. Equally, when the ultra-secular cadres of Pol Pot carry State socialism into the world with literal and bloody logic we are witnesses to a fundamentalist storm-centre. Not every expression of fundamentalism ends with the execution of the other. When James Jones persuaded his followers to leave their worldly life behind in California and set up an utopia in distant Guyana, there was implicit in this an absolutist confidence. When the confidence disintegrated, there was nothing left to live or die for. It becomes more understandable why 900 or so adherents of the People's Temple allowed their oath of obedience to extend to swallowing deadly poison *en masse*, on instruction by Jones. Perhaps Reverend Moon's Unification Church in the United States and the large number of *ashrams* following extremist *gurus* from India have not exerted quite so dominating a hold on their faithful, but they draw to the fold many of those wanderers who will pay virtually any personal price to be given a sense of purpose in life. There are countless further examples of how this quest for identity is being perverted or put in the service of horrifying missions.

Of course, it is also evident that we live at a time when certain bonds of oppression have been lifted. The great popular struggles against fascism in Europe and the Pacific ended in victory, and after World War II the rise of non-Western peoples against colonialism did engender a sense of potency for many ordinary people and positive outcomes of these struggles are experienced even today. In Europe, guaranteed employment and a minimum standard of living became basic material rights, at least until somewhat abridged in the 1970s; and remain so in Eastern Europe. In the last few years, Spain, Greece, Portugal, Argentina, Haiti and the Philippines have

Introduction

re-established parliamentary democracy. There is an upsurge of struggle in South Africa and support for the anti-apartheid movement grows throughout the world.

But there have also emerged into view numerous festering wounds. The world has never been constituted by natural political communities, nor by relations of equality and mutuality among distinct communities. The State is never coterminus with the boundaries of a natural political community. Sometimes the State manages to embody a compromise among its distinct societal elements, as was the case in Lebanon before the civil war of 1975 or, as in India, until ethnic strife has intensified in recent years. But compromises are fragile when passions are intense or manipulated by a variety of internal and external forces. Often the apparatus of the State is captured by the representatives of a given political majority (or by a powerful and oppressing minority as in South Africa), securing for its members a disproportionate share of rewards in terms of economic, political, and cultural resources. The 'inferior' communities feel abused and must be coerced into acquiescence. In situations of overall hardship, the circumstances of the inferior communities can become intolerable. Resistance of some kind, however desperate, is often undertaken. Repression is thereby invited, generating still more resistance, and an upward spiral of political violence is underway. Without a genuinely just and fair treatment for individuals and groups, the intensity of conflict between the State and a portion of society is almost assured, given contemporary awareness that oppressive conditions are not justifiable. The protracted struggle of the Basques in Spain, the Nagas and Mizos in India, Tibetans in China, the Shans and Karens in Burma, the Timorese in Indonesia and the Kurds in Iran, Iraq and Turkey bear witness to the reality that even a small, regionally restricted natural community cannot be easily pacified by the instruments available to the modern State.

In some circumstances, the colonial order, or other forms of authoritarian rule, bottled up tensions among communities, froze them in time. But the removal of the colonial masters released the subsidiary horizontal tensions contained within the State's often artificial boundaries. Tribal and racial resentments long held in check erupted with fury, often serving the fortunes of calculating politicians. The campaigns against the Asian merchant families in East Africa, or even more so, the bitter campaigns of popular terror against the Chinese in Indonesia and lately against the Tamils in Sri Lanka convey a sense of the depth and pervasiveness of these lethal tensions. There are many peoples facing the dreadful possibility of genocidal campaigns directed against them by the managers of State power.

The post-colonial State had hoped for some measure of economic development amid such turbulence. But capital and technology continued to remain out of its reach. More importantly, a re-colonisation of elite minds in these 'liberated States' has been manifest in the desire to imitate the lifestyles and consumerism of the former colonial masters. This impulse is reinforced by multinational corporations, banks, global institutions and a variety of materialist creeds that are the Mephistopheles of our time, tempting and enticing the Third World, while imposing sinister new types of bondage in exchange. Inappropriate technologies, misconceived priorities in terms of public and private investment, alien concepts and techniques and, underneath, a false conviction that massive human engineering, of which militarisation is an essential component, are needed and even desirable during the State-building era.

In the background of this restructuring of world politics in the post-colonial era is the failure of the main political ideologies to fulfill expectations. Liberalism with its faith in the individual and in the limited State was not able to offer much consolation in circumstances of mass poverty and discontent. The stress on economic growth which promised to make a country—mainly its elite—strong and prosperous tended to turn its productive energies over to capitalist or State-capitalist forces; little effort was devoted to satisfying the needs of the poor, that is, of 90 per cent or more of many countries. Since that is the case, the class base of the governing process is obvious, and is bound eventually to produce a revolutionary situation that is often deferred and disguised by reliance on the terrorist capabilities of the State—swift, efficient and ruthless.

Liberalism fails also in the First World. Increasingly, the technology of war, particularly nuclear war, is incompatible with political democracy of a genuine kind. The required permanent readiness

Introduction

for war, with mobilised resources and an intelligence operation that provides leaders with secret assessments of impending danger, necessarily removes citizens, and even representative institutions, from the governing processes. This removal is further assured by a military bureaucracy that 'knows best' when it comes to national security and opposes all forms of popular scrutiny. In effect, the various elements of representative democracy are being increasingly coopted by the militarised sectors of the modern State; political parties and elected politicians are required to carry on their operations within preset boundaries. Citizens have been converted into subjects when it comes to national security. And the definition of national security is an ever-expanding one that reaches deep down into the sinews of domestic life and also involves defence against external danger.

On the other side of the ideological equation is the socialist experience. When mass discontent gets mobilised and launches an armed struggle that results in violence, the socialist State is confronted with a different kind of problem. Safeguarding the revolution justifies, even necessitates, a deepening militarisation. If militarisation persists over the years, a revolutionary State is distanced from its own people. Secrecy pervades even routine operations of the socialist States. Personnel and policy changes are kept well removed from popular scrutiny and even events in the outside world are carefully filtered by a tightly regimented media before they reach the people.

The transformation of Marxist thinking also explains this drift into statist rule over society. The whole analysis by which a State is defined as exploitative if, and only if, it is dominated by feudal or capitalist exploiters, makes the ideology defenceless against a State dominated by the vanguard of the oppressed. In this respect, the official Marxist-Leninist belief that a socialist State is by definition the vanguard of the peace movement can lead officials to brand independent peace activists as 'criminals'. Such results are the consequence of naively assuming that any concentration of power in the hands of a supposedly progressive class is not liable to be grossly abused. Yet, gross abuses of power have taken place in socialist States and have been admitted as such by successive regimes in the Soviet Union, China, and some East European countries.

These various dangers are reinforced by the interplay of ideologies at the international level. The competition of ideologies partially masks conflicts among rival power-centres for resources and spheres of influence, that is, old-time *geopolitik*. The ideological rivalry also helps mobilise tensions and fears which provide leaders with a pliable domestic atmosphere. The military technology and strategic doctrine of the adversary are relied upon by both sides in the rivalry to justify constant vigilance and protection against the 'enemy' who may not pose much of an actual threat, being more worried about the costs and consequences of war and preoccupied with upholding the *status quo*.

The basic world historical situation can be summarised thus: a series of pressures from above and below have tended to militarise the State, its conception of government and external relations; this militarisation has occurred in a context of technologies of scale and vast potential for devastation and in a setting beset by ecological, economic, social and cultural distress and acute societal grievance; as a result, multi-faceted conflicts and civil strife are rampant; to sustain order in such circumstances has meant internal repression and permanent readiness for major wars; these processes and structures imperil the future relationship between State and society, between society and nature, and damage the overall quality of interaction within the assembly of States.

We are left with an overarching question. Is there a way out? The paragraphs that follow do no more than anticipate some possible lines of response. We make no claims to have cleared a path that can lead humanity safely to the future. We know that a variety of path-clearing projects are underway, many of them at the grassroots and therefore largely unknown. Our concern is to point some of them out. Our hope is that several of these paths will be used by larger numbers frequently enough and that those who travel along their course will gain in confidence and capability. In the end, emergent social forces need to reclaim control over their destiny, not by negating the State or technology or ideologies but by transforming these in liberating directions, strengthening their life-giving potential, while weakening their capacities and dispositions towards

Introduction

dominance, exploitation and destruction. We think and act on the firm conviction that such possibilities can be realised or, at the very least, that movement in these restorative directions can occur, and that such movement will establish new horizons of aspirations. It is by moving toward goals in support of real social tensions and counter-tendencies that we affirm our faith in humanity, not by unfurling one more blueprint that could be superimposed, *deus ex machina*, by a like-minded leadership.

The affirmation that underlies our concern takes its stand on the terrain of society and political community. If the State and technology are seen as derivations justified only to the extent that they serve the purposes of society and political community, then a start can be made on the crucial task of informing thought and understanding with an innovative, alternative orientation, framework and vision. As we see it, the State and technology originally emerged out of human needs and wants, in different forms, at given times, for particular ends. It is to these two interlinked dimensions of the *problematique* of peace and transformation that we now turn.

Role of the State

In the present epoch of history, we tend to forget that the institution of the State was a human creation to meet human needs. The State was liberating to the extent that it provided greater assurance to societies and communities against disorganised violence and could channelise productive energies and cultural creativity for constructive purposes, including a lessening of the impact of scarcity on the quality of human existence. The State promised defence of territory against war and/or criminality and also over-saw the market so that trading in what was desirable could take place. Above all, the State, in recent times, undertook to correct or contain the inequities inherent in antecedent or emergent social traditions and structures, relying on more general notions of minimum decency.

Despite these historic liberating functions, however, the State in its essence remains a system dedicated to political domination and control. The relations of domination, of course, take different forms; the State dominates through consent and, failing that, through coercion, usually through both. The State rarely is a monolith; it is a set of institutions such as the legislature, the civil bureaucracy, the judiciary, the armed forces and the like. These institutions act sometimes in competition, sometimes in concert; sometimes by asserting diverse autonomies and sometimes by one institution undermining all the others. The balance among and within them, their internal structure and their differential relations with various forces in society shape the particular character of a given State, whether it becomes liberator or oppressor, whether it responds to or ignores popular feelings, whether it transforms itself or stagnates.

In modern political communities, even the non-governmental political forces are largely constituted in relation to the State. Political parties, citizens' groups, trade unions, grassroot movements, indeed virtually all political struggles are organised to gain access to the different institutions of the State or have impact on its policies and pronouncements. Quite obviously, the most dominant of the groups have privileged access, again obviously, at the expense of those that lack weight. In the overwhelming majority of the Third World countries the dominant groups seek and often secure outright denial of access to almost all those outside the charmed circle. Under such circumstances, the State's promise of liberation has been almost totally betrayed.

Popular access to the institutions of the State entered a new phase after World War II in the advanced industrialised countries of the West. There the new project of the State was to combine welfare and security. It was believed that humane and managed capitalism within the framework of a collective security system could bring social stability and material and humanising benefits for all. The liberal capitalist economy relying on redistribution through taxation and growing equality of opportunity could produce both guns and butter, and thereby achieve high degrees of stability and contentment. And the formula did work for three decades following 1945. The advanced industrial societies of the West saw unprecedented prosperity for all during the sixties and early seventies. They also became militarily unrivalled, economically powerful, and served as models for other societies.

In the socialist States, the experience of the 1930s and 1940s

Introduction

seemed to show that the system of central planning and effective management by the State could yield accelerated and sustainable rates of economic growth as well as a strong security system. In this scheme, popular accesss to the institutions of the State played only a minor role; the people were considered, or at least said to be, too vulnerable to corrupting influences from the West and to capitalist and imperialist forces generally, undermining the 'gains of the Revolution'. In this period, the socialist formula also performed successfully. The socialist States of the East registered impressive growth rates during the 1950s and 1960s and also produced extremely powerful military systems which safeguarded their revolutions against threats from within and without.

The leaders of the newly decolonised nation-States of the Third World drew their inspiration from different patterns of emphasis from both models. Most generally, they sought to combine managed capitalism, centralised planning and equitable distribution in their development policies. Popular access to the institutions of the State was often 'managed' but generally not excluded. This project too initially yielded impressive results. The economies of these new States showed high growth rates, with some attention to distribution as well, and the national military systems were getting stronger and stronger. In many cases, popular participation in the affairs of the State was also manifestly on the increase.

The consensus needed to execute these projects of the State was not achieved without struggle. With the coming of the Cold War in the late 1940s and 1950s, political dissent was either marginalised or suppressed. In the advanced industrial countries of the West this was done through a dominant ideology tailored against the so-called communist threat; this culminated in the highly repressive phase of McCarthyism. In the socialist countries of the East, Stalinist terror did the job. Elsewhere in the Third World countries, dissent was suppressed through a whole variety of action ranging from simple coercion to physical extermination. In short, implementation of the new projects of the State initially went hand in hand with suppression of dissent through various means in different systems. As the gains of the post-war period were registered, consent for State activity grew, and during the 1960s and 1970s, at least in Western countries, dissenting activities were not much of a threat and were easily tolerated. Hence it is fair to say that during this period the State system in advanced industrial countries became, in some respects, more liberal and tolerant.

The domestic projects of these diverse categories of States required a new international State system. The United States and the Soviet Union, the two most powerful of the States, each sought to shape the global order to satisfy their grand designs. The United States organised a series of collective security systems like NATO, CENTO, SEATO, ANZUS, and the Rio treaty involving countries from different parts of the world, including some in the Third World. It also built up an international economic system based on the US dollar and largely controlled a network of international institutions like the International Monetary Fund, the General Agreement on Trade and Tariffs (GATT) and the World Bank. The collective security systems and the dollar system taken together led to a distinctive global hegemony that turned out to be far more powerful and pervasive than any other single colonial system in world history. It was a global system of political domination which used a variety of instruments ranging from consent, aid or bribery, to coercion and even outright military intervention.

The Soviet-led socialist countries excluded themselves from this global system. The Soviet Union sought to protect its bloc from the military and economic expansion of the Western powers. It formed a parallel security system, consisting of the socialist countries of Eastern Europe, the Republic of Mongolia, China, and later, North Korea, North Vietnam and Cuba, with the Soviet Union as the pivot. But the Soviet Union was not able to provide a sufficiently strong economic system since the rouble was so much weaker than the US dollar and the bases for mutual trade were much more limited. Internal cohesion within the 'bloc' was maintained through the party system, through the public security system, and if necessary through military intervention. Such controls were legitimised by invoking the threat of the US global system. In turn, the US system also legitimised itself by invoking the threat from the Soviet 'global' system; the 'global' element was the Moscow-centred discipline of some Communist parties in some Western countries and the Marxist-

Introduction

oriented insurgent groups elsewhere in the world.

Those who remained outside the two global frameworks did not escape the constraining impacts of the new paradigm of the State. Whatever variant of the system a particular government adopted, the fundamental point of departure was material accumulation or economic growth which was to be achieved through technological progress whether indirectly promoted by the State or achieved through the direct intervention of the State and its agencies.

It was technological progress of a definite type. A fundamental weakness of the State's new paradigm was the view that technology was somehow abstract, exogenous, one might almost say God-given, and that its maximal application was necessarily progressive. The term used by economists, 'manna from heaven', expressed a much deeper social consensus, at least in advanced industrial countries. The consensus was that the reliance on Western science would necessarily benefit mankind, and at the same time science was somehow beyond human analysis and control. In fact, the consensus, and the cock-sure form it took, was based on a specific 'success story'. It was based on the type of technological progress that was peculiarly the product of the social circumstances of the United States in the 1930s and 1940s. It was technological progress directed towards two types of demand: military power and final consumption. It was especially inspired by the American experience in automobile production —the mass production techniques pioneered by Henry Ford. And it depended on the abundance of cheap energy, above all, oil.

It was this model of technological prowess that most States adopted after World War II. It was a globally shared State project: material accumulation via the spread of what one might describe for convenience as the American technology culture; we shall refer to it as the post-war technology paradigm. It was this paradigm that imposed a kind of global unity on industrial enclaves and military institutions everywhere: the spread of roads and airfields, of Coca Cola and cinemas, of refrigerators, washing machines and fast food, of tanks and bombers and missiles. It was a project that brought benefits for many and disbenefits for others. In the service of this project, States in many different parts of the world adopted a common strategy. States tended to promote the use of petroleum at the expense of other sources of energy; energy conservation was totally neglected. In market economies, private transportation was promoted at the cost of public transportation. In time, these preferences began to distort the priorities in not only the centrally planned but the 'mixed' economies as well. In many instances, State policies were tilted in favour of military build-ups and consumerism, neglecting the production of social goods and the protection of the environment. These preferences were built into the structure of the State itself: in the institutional balance between departments of defence and arms manufacturers, or between departments of energy and oil companies; in the ideologies of the ruling political parties and the pattern of political patronage; in the hegemony of particular research institutes or universities; in the allocation of State funds for research and education. And in the centrally planned economies, where State influence was even more pervasive, the phenomenon of what is sometimes known as the input-output conservatism of government bureaucrats led to many types of rigidity.

Sometime in the late 1960s, the growth potential of the post-war technology paradigm began to reach its limits. Markets for automobiles became saturated, energy supplies became less abundant; what are known as diseconomies—environmental degradation, individual discontent, societal distress—became more obvious. Only the military market, which could never re-enter the civilian economy, continued to expand unchecked by any reactive forces. Because of the dominant global role of the United States, the ramifications of the faltering American economy were felt throughout the world. This was the essence of the economic crisis. It was a crisis of material accumulation, a failure of both production and distribution in relation to the globally shared State project. The crisis was initially expressed in the slow-down in the growth of US productivity that began in the late 1960s. The possibility of adopting new forms of technological progress that might, for example, be directed towards food production, energy conservation, renewable sources of energy, resource recycling, environmental protection, constructive use of new discoveries in micro-electronics and biotechnology, was inhibited by the structural dominance of the post-war technology paradigm and the expressed preferences of the global State system. By

Introduction

the 1970s, economic growth in a number of Western industrial countries showed a negative trend. Something similar happened in socialist countries as well. The State policies of the late 1940s and 1950s had succeeded in achieving 'extensive' accumulation at a rapid pace. But the same policies, once the available labour and natural resources had been fully absorbed, did not continue through the decades. What was needed was 'intensive' accumulation through growth in productivity. But this needed continuous innovation which the central planning system was simply unable to generate.

Perhaps this phase of economic stagnation has now begun to pass away. Capitalism has proven its resilience, as has the State framework to its international field of operations. By curtailing welfare policies and priming still further the military pump, the United States has experienced a kind of economic recovery under conservative auspices. Growth is up, the dollar is strong, inflation is way down; but deficits at home and abroad make the adjustment fragile, especially when associated with the overburdened world financial system and the risks of debt repudiation and bankruptcy arising from the world debt structure.

All the while military expenditures have continued to rise. Most Western governments have adopted more or less brutal methods for limiting wage rises because productivity growth cannot keep up with growth of wages, and so, consumerist expectations are frustrated. The economic crises in the socialist States, even if not always as acute as those in the capitalist States, also show the failure of the State to meet the expectations of the citizens.

The only States that have partially escaped the trap of stagnation in innovation have been those which avoided the burden of the arms race—West Germany and Japan. But now that the United States has exerted pressures to make these economic challengers share more fully in the costs of the military preparedness of the US-led global system, some of their industries may suffer a fate similar to that of the American industry in the future.

In the tradition-bound Third World countries, the new technological project of the State has met its greatest set-backs. It ended up establishing large military machines for the State in many countries and higher levels of consumption for the elites; the basic needs of the people were almost totally neglected. One set of critical consequences has involved a series of severe cultural and social dislocations. But such is the hegemony of the belief in technological progress that all indigenous alternatives are contemptuously dismissed by the State and its agencies. The mindless search for technology-transfer has added to the already staggering debt burdens while 'export-led economic growth' suffered badly for a while due to the economic crisis in the industrial States. The State in the Third World has, for the most part, failed to bring about technological progress and has, in the process, created deeper poverty and destitution; it has engaged in wholesale violation of human rights and visited cultural destruction upon its peoples. Of course, the record of gains and losses is complex, and some States, most notably the Asian NICs, have registered impressive economic gains, but under rather special and artificial circumstances.

In spite of obvious progress in some areas, the State in many parts of the world has, as a result of broken promises and outright failures, increasingly come to be looked upon as oppressor rather than liberator. The earlier consensus on which the success of the State's new project was based has now broken down. Dissent is no longer on the margins of societies. Unemployed youth or workers threatened with joblessness in the West, regimented workers and intellectuals in the East and the impoverished urban middle classes and vast masses of the poor in the South are the new emerging forces. As a result, the deprived and oppressed in the Third World now form the backbone of dissent and resistance against the State. The response of leaders who wield State power to rising dissent from below has been a mixture of populist rhetoric, media manipulation, coercion and, on occasion, outright suppression. But the trend is unmistakably clear; it is a shift from techniques of obtaining consent to techniques of effective coercion. Coercion can take many forms; it can be economic, political or military or, more likely, some combination of all three. The United States, to sustain the postwar international economic system and the role of the dollar, as well as to manipulate popular expectations of rising living standards, has been practising economic coercion in the form of monetarist policies at home. Additionally it is promoting them elsewhere

Introduction

through international financial institutions. These practices are supplemented with interest-rate wars, trade warfare, tariffs and other devices of economic policy. Political coercion in Western countries generally comes in the form of restricting the people's access to the State through grants of greater powers to the police, and by restrictions on popular demonstrations. The use of intelligence agencies against political dissidents is also important. Political coercion in the East uses more or less the same techniques to suppress any deviation whatsoever from the 'line' ordained by the central authorities. And in many Third World countries the armoury of techniques of political coercion includes 'emergency' powers, suspension of fundamental rights, detention without trial and in some cases permanent autocracy facilitated by martial law.

Western countries tend to practise military coercion largely only against other countries. But the use of the military against domestic dissidence is not unknown. The use of the British Army in Northern Ireland and the Spanish Army's actions against the Basque Liberation Movement are prominent recent examples. In the countries of the East, the armed forces have the specific task of "defending the gains of the Revolution" and this task is often extended to defending the gains of revolutions in other countries as well. Afghanistan illustrates the extension of such an interventionary approach to a Third World country. In large parts of the Third World, the State almost routinely uses military coercion against its own dissident population; in some cases the military and the State become co-terminus.

All these developments have made the State increasingly vulnerable to attacks from both old and new forces. The old forces have always opposed the liberating role of the State, distrusted the new technological project of the State and have wanted to minimise the role of the State in society. They have now reappeared, often in the form of new right-wing movements and new religious fundamentalist sects. Many aim at the seizure of State power. The supreme example of this is the Iranian revolution. But elsewhere such sects and movements go under the name of 'moral volunteers', 'defence of Hindus', Moral Majority. When such right-wing forces take over the State, ostensibly to overcome the wrongs, they often transform the State into something which is even worse than the *ancien regime*.

The new forces challenging the State are a variety of grassroot movements, the peace and 'green' movements in the North and an array of social movements in the South campaigning for civil and democratic rights, tribal survival, a fair deal for the peasant, against exploitation from the urban centres, protection of forests and indigenous ways of living against destructive industrialisation, indeed, against 'development' as the presiding elites define it. In addition, workers' struggles, like those of the miners in Britain, have re-emerged in a new form as social emancipation movements that are far wider in their scope than traditional economistic struggles. In parts of the Third World, too, new and radical forms of trade unionism, including the so-called unorganised sector, are emerging. Increasingly, these are seen as part of the new grassroot movements. The grassroot movements demand a transformation of the State, a shift in the institutional balance of the State so that social needs can take priority over military needs and wasteful consumption. Usually, without aiming at the seizure of State power they demand greater public accountability and new mechanisms for access to the State. But they also seek to halt the centralising and expanding thrust of the State and create alternative areas for the people's involvement and a new public discourse, in the process recapturing the autonomous zones and initiatives within society that have been usurped by the State.

Both in the North and the South, these movements draw their main support from those who have been progressively excluded from the political process and have been frustrated in their attempts to influence what appears to them as a disastrous course taken by the State. The inability to do anything at all about the State in the North building up an omnicidal nuclear war capability is one example of their despair. Similarly, the helplessness with which they must watch millions dying a slow death through hunger, disease and oppression illustrates the anguish and limits of the movements in the South. The Bhopal catastrophe contains within its reality many of these frustrations and what is concretely implied by the absence of popular control.

Just as the State emerged in response to human needs, the

grassroot movements, too, have come into being in response to the new human needs which the State has failed to satisfy. However, there are crucial differences between the two. The State has all the resources of the society at its command; indeed, it has far more. The State often has the resources of other States also available to it, depending on the ideological, political and military links it has with other States. In contrast, the grassroot movements have, at best, access only to local resources and that too in competition with the State. Because of its long history, the State has the ideology, the organisation, the legitimacy (or at least some vestiges of legitimacy) and, above all, the brute power to sustain itself in the face of challenge. The grassroot movements are in their infancy, they are fragmented and isolated, they are a *mélange* of competing and contradictory ideologies and, above all, they lack power; all they have is their resolve and, on occasions, public opinion. Grassroot movements thus find themselves engaged in an unequal struggle against the State.

Why then do we look upon the grassroot movements—with some exceptions as we make clear later—as the new historical force for the transformation of the State and indeed for achieving peace with transformation? The ongoing struggles at the grassroots are not mini-Jaqueries which burst forth and peter out. As a global phenomenon they show a remarkable staying power. It is true that they have risen in response to local and regional consequences of global problems such as frustration with the role of the State, militarisation, especially the arms race, the economic crisis, conflicts over natural resources, violations of human rights, destruction of cultures and misconceived and misapplied science and technology. But unlike in earlier times, the movements are coming to realise the complex interconnections among these problems even at the local level. This is why the concerns of these movements and their support bases in society have been widening, even though at a slow pace, with the passage of time, and adopting a transnational orientation. The 'greens' of the North no longer struggle only for ecological renewal but take up the issues of peace, women's rights, protection for indigenous peoples, and the transformation of the State. Similarly, many movements struggling for the right to livelihood within the South are becoming aware of interlinkages between economic deprivation and the State's development policies, the role of technology, the scramble for natural resources, and especially the bewildering trends and counter-trends associated with militarisation. And they interrelate in this manner because these trends represent new historical forces—against specialisation of knowledge and segmentation of life on which so much faith was placed since the industrial revolution in the West, but which have brought humanity to a point of growing discord and potential disintegration.

What these movements lack is a coherent shared theory which illuminates hidden interlinkages in clear and understandable terms, a theory which, moreover, serves as a guide and frame in their daily struggles, and takes its shape from these struggles. It is only such a theory and new organisational forms which will enable them to join hands not only across local spaces but across State borders as well. Without such underpinnings, the prospects of future generations are diminished; ultimately, these movements are emerging as guardians of the future even when this role is not part of their explicit programme. The purpose of our effort is to contribute, along with many others who are engaged in the daily struggles for peace with transformation, to the discovery and articulation of such a theory.

2
Militarisation: The Imaginary War

Introduction
It is recognised by an increasing number of people in the world that peace cannot be a mere absence of war. The depressing reality is that millions of people are victims of malnutrition and starvation every year and the number of starving people is likely to increase unless the present trend is reversed. Thus, it is evident that the opposite of 'peace' is not war alone but violence which includes the structural deprivations of the present system that give rise to chronic slow starvation on a massive scale, widespread atrocities on the landless and the other poor and repressive and genocidal acts of some governments against ethnic minorities.

We would like to establish a direct relationship between organised violence and militarisation. We should first distinguish between ordinary, random violence and organised violence. The latter arises out of underlying conflicts, both intranational and international, and involves the use of physical coercion in relations between individuals and institutions. As conflicts intensify so does the tendency to resort to violence and to the propensity of the States themselves to become more and more violent. To the extent that the States increasingly rely on violence, societies can be said to become increasingly militarised. We thus define militarisation in a broad sense as socially organised physical coercion, and it is in this sense that we believe it is fruitful to analyse the militarisation process which is under way on a global scale, encompassing East and West, North and South, embracing a variety of dimensions that gives rise to organised violence.

Seen from this perspective, it is a secondary question whether the agents of coercion are the military, the paramilitary, the police or the intelligence agencies. There are ostensibly 'civilian' governments which are as repressive as, or even more repressive than, some of the military regimes. Armaments, not the military as such, do indeed constitute the cardinal component of the means of coercion, and can be considered to be one of the useful indicators of militarisation. But armaments can be appropriate indicators only so long as they are analysed in the broader context of underlying conflict. We, therefore, think it imperative to examine critically the political structure of the present world order which generates the processes of militarisation and concomitant armament dynamics.

Of course, physical coercion has historically characterised all known State systems. But the particular forms of physical coercion have varied enormously according to time and place. Indeed the clash of different forms of physical coercion in wars between different societies was, historically, one of the main ways in which different societies learnt from each other.

Perhaps the most striking feature of the modern epoch is the homogeneity of forms of physical coercion. Armed forces, police forces, paramilitary forces around the world make use of much the same type of military technology, largely manufactured in the United States and the Soviet Union and a handful of other advanced industrial countries. With the help of advisors and training courses, forms of command, patterns of operations, methods of recruitment also bear a marked global resemblance. For the first time in history, soldiers or policemen from different societies have more in common with each other than the societies from which they come. In a sense, it could be said that the institutions of militarisation represent an extreme form of the post-war technology paradigm. Weapons systems —ships, aircraft, armoured vehicles, missiles—have developed in a more or less linear evolution from the weapons of World War II. They are products, by and large, of automobile and aerospace establishments; they are more energy intensive than other kinds of products; they require roads, airfields and modern communications.

Militarisation: The Imaginary War

The process of militarisation imposes a kind of military-technical unity on the world which is in stark contrast to the diversity in economic, political and especially cultural spheres. Militarisation is a coercive process, not simply because it represents potential or actual physical coercion, but because, in its specific historical guise, it refuses diversity.

Forms of Militarisation

We have defined militarisation as all forms of socially organised physical coercion. War is an important subcomponent of this definition. War is socially organised physical coercion against a similarly organised opponent. In general, war is between States. But civil war could be described as war between a State and a proto-State, in that guerilla forces have generally established some form of political organisation together with military organisation, i.e. its own form of organised physical coercion. By and large, war is the terrain of the armed forces. Military spending represents a measure, albeit often inaccurate, of the resources devoted to war-making. The other form of organised physical coercion is internal repression. This may be used against a politically organised opponent but not necessarily an opponent organised for violence; the opponent may be organised for non-violent action as, for instance, the Indian national movement or the Western peace movement. Or it may be used to simply suppress an emerging social force, based either on class or on other social bonds like caste, language, or nationality. Disorganised violence may also occur, e.g., brick throwing during student riots or ethnic riots. These forms of physical coercion are by and large the terrain of the security forces, paramilitary forces, etc. Many of the generalisations it is possible to make about the conditions for increased militarisation and about the structure of militarisation and the way in which this structure is influenced by the militarisation of the dominant Powers, apply to both forms. But war-making has certain particular characteristics, e.g. the role of the armed forces.

The primary role of the armed forces is for war. And war in our world is on the increase. According to Ruth Sivard, there have been 105 major wars (with deaths of 1000 or more) since 1945. In the 1950s, the number of wars per year averaged nine. In the 1960s, this rose to 11 and, in the 1970s and so far in the 1980s, wars have averaged 14 per year. Moreover, wars appear to be becoming more and more destructive. The war in El Salvador has so far claimed some 50,000 lives, or one person in a 100. One aeroplane carrying the cluster-type munitions used by Israel in Lebanon is equivalent to a Lance missile with a single 1 kiloton nuclear warhead.

These wars have taken place almost exclusively in the Third World. Depending on how one defines the Soviet interventions in Hungary and Czechoslovakia, or the continuing violence in Northern Ireland, it may be said that the advanced industrial countries have had almost no experience of actual war on their territories since 1945. Nevertheless, their armed forces have a political and ideological role. They claim to be, in a literal sense, defenders of the nation which is identified with a collectivity of nations, e.g. the 'free world' or the socialist world, whose definitions are often imposed by those who define these collectivities, more often than not in a bid for global domination. It is only by exploring this political or ideological role that we can understand why the advanced industrial countries, despite the absence of actual war, are much more heavily militarised, measured in terms of State resources devoted to physical coercion, than Third World countries.

In advanced industrial countries, militarisation is justified by deterrence—the need to prepare for war in order to avoid war. 'Deterrence' can be described as a kind of imaginary war. In military exercises, scenarios of war planners, in the rhetoric of the political leaders, war is played out daily in our minds. It is this kind of psychological spectacle that helps to determine perceptions of political power both between States and within particular societies. The most recent U.S. proposals to take the arms race into space can be understood in this way. The Strategic Defence Initiative ('Star Wars') is a new offensive in the battle to control the global imagination. Its proponents are fond of pointing out that they are bringing peace to the heavens and establishing peace on earth. By combining the modern experience of computers and video games with traditional fantasies, 'Star Wars' can be viewed as an attempt to re-establish beliefs about American pre-eminence. But it is worth noting that, at least in the minds of the military planners, the imaginary war has much more in common with World War II, primarily as it was fought in Europe, than it has with what we know as nuclear war. It can be further argued that the prevailing form of militarisation—the missions, the weapons, the organisation of military units—owes much to the experience of World War II, a period which represented the zenith of American technology. It was then that the dominant automobile and aerospace companies entered the military business; Henry Ford's production techniques were applied throughout American industry. It was then that the Soviet Union learned, through lend-lease and the experience of war, the potential of the new technology. Above all it was that period that entrenched the belief that the achievements of science and technology were dazzling and limitless.

Whatever the relevance of that exposure, it remains a basis of globally determined criteria for perceived military strength. A nation is considered to be militarily powerful if it possesses weapons systems that would do well in the imaginary war in Europe. According to the imaginary war, numbers of weapons and sophistication, measured by a set of widely accepted criteria that were considered important in World War II—speed, payload, guidance etc.—are what is required. Nuclear weapons have special importance. Both domestically and internationally, countries are awarded a place on the perceived military—and presumably political—hierarchy according to these criteria.

These perceptions, and indeed the memory of World War II, are so widespread precisely because of the pervasive influence of the armed forces, the arms industry and strategic think tanks. The armed forces represent one of the most important institutions of the State and their role vis-a-vis other institutions—the civil service or Parliament or party—can determine the balance of State priorities and the direction of State policies. With minor exceptions, in almost all countries, regardless of the political systems, the military enjoy considerable influence in determining their own portion of the budget. Among the great military powers, moreover, the armament enterprises have a dominant industrial role and their requirements generate pressure for further militarisation. In technology too they provide both a laboratory and the arena of implementing the latest.

It should be stressed that the memory of World War II is in fact continuously shaped by the military and industrial institutions. The US strategic emphasis, for example, is as much a consequence of a bureaucratic victory of the airforce and aerospace industry over the army as it is a consequence of actual military experience. The resemblance of the imaginary war to World War II stems from the fact that these institutions were, by and large, created in World War II. It is their memory that persists. The reality of Hiroshima and Nagasaki, for example, is relegated to near oblivion.

It is also the case that the influence of the military and military industrial institutions in both advanced industrial and Third World countries spreads beyond their own concerns. In particular, because the armed forces have a vested interest in the appropriate infrastructure to develop, produce, operate and maintain modern weapons systems and to enlist appropriate skills for the same, they tend to develop definite ideas about modes of development linked to the post-war technology paradigm. For example, military technology depends on oil, hence the military tend to support oil-oriented energy priorities. This is particularly important in the Third World where the appropriate infrastructure may not exist. Putting such an infrastructure in place then becomes a high priority for security which in turn forces a particular direction and place for 'development'. Although the armed forces in the Third World have displayed a wide range of political positions, from radical to conservative, they tend to share a partiality for rapid industrialisation based on the post-war technology paradigm. In Latin America, this concern has been institutionalised in the National Security Doctrine which advocates an advance of national power *per se*, and in which the armed forces, as experts in national security, are seen as agents of this advance. In order to guarantee 'development', which alone is presumed to ensure this, the military may often intervene and try to control the other institutions of the State, particularly through military coups.

Ruth Sivard has defined a country under military control according to the following criteria: key political leadership by military officers; existence of a state of martial law; extra-judicial authority exercised by security forces; lack of central political control over

Militarisation: The Imaginary War

large sections of the country where official or unofficial security forces rule; control by foreign military forces. According to these criteria, she finds 56 of the 114 countries classified as 'developing' are under military control. (This includes Turkey, but not, of course, Poland.)

But the armed forces have other political roles which may be encouraged by civilian authorities. They have an ideological role both domestically and internationally. Displays of strength through army parades, and other spectacles, the aquisition of new advanced military technology, etc., serve at once to intimidate through fear of war or fear of the enemy, and to evoke nationalist sentiment and pride. In Europe and the Pacific, the imaginary East-West war serves as a disciplining force in both blocs justifying the military alliance systems, marginalising opposition by bracketing it with the imaginary enemy and mobilising popular support for coercive policies. In the Third World, regional enemies, however real or imaginary the conflict, can serve the same domestic purposes. Hence India's continuing emphasis on the threat from Pakistan, or earlier from China. And the same with Pakistan. The armed forces also have a disciplining role in society that stems from their own internal structure. The spread of militaristic culture is also an indirect form of coercion that has proved immensely important for some countries in the early part of this century, or later in South Korea or Taiwan and even in some socialist countries. This militaristic culture is manifested in the display of medals and uniforms or military forms of command in civilian situations, in an emphasis on heroism and in the constant replay of past military victories in books and films and cartoon strips. Conscription and military-patriotic education in schools are ways of socialising young minds into this culture.

In practice, the perceptions of military strength, based on an imaginary war, are regularly disproved in actual war. According to the criteria for military strength established in this imaginary war, the US ought quickly to have won the war in Vietnam; the Arab States ought easily to have defeated Israel. In the two Indo-Pakistan wars, the sophisticated military equipment provided to Pakistan by the United States did not live up to the hopes reposed in it. The Indian Gnat, designed in Britain in 1959, turned out to be the more effective. In the current Gulf war, Iran and Iraq have had difficulty in operating modern aircraft and missiles. These experiences are, however, said to be irrelevant to the main contingency which the developers and producers of military equipment expect to face, namely a war in Europe or a global strategic war. The armed forces in the US and the Soviet Union are internally structured around the prospect of an East-West war. Yet, via various forms of military assistance, and the general conditioning that goes with specific hardware and technology this kind of thinking has influenced the structure of the armed forces in Third World countries as well. Armed forces have, therefore, a vested institutional interest in some universal war, in this case modelled after an imaginary East-West War. Hence the continuing influence of military doctrines and technology developed in the North on countries in the South. Since armed forces influence perceptions of military technology, and indirectly of technology in general, technology serves in a circular fashion to uphold their political role. However, increasing militarisation is an expression of increasing structural violence which also increases the tendency for *actual* war. It is in the contradiction between the political and military roles of militarisation that opportunities for demilitarisation arise, that is, provided larger social movements take root and redefine political and transformative roles.

The Process of Militarisation

Modern history, dominated by the history of western material civilisation, can be seen as a process through which the late-starters who have been disadvantaged have attempted to close-in on the early starters—and hence the advantaged—who have vested interests in maintaining the military, political, economic or cultural superiority gained by them. In the 19th century, the position of superiority held by Great Britain as the guardian of world order (*Pax Britannica*) was challenged by Germany (Prussia). When Germany succeeded in closing in on France, the Franco-Prussian war broke out. The international regime installed by the Versailles Settlement was challenged by Germany, Italy, and Japan (the Axis Powers) which undertook an abortive attempt to close-in on Anglo-American and West European early starters with the result that World War II broke out.

Militarisation: The Imaginary War

The United States emerged from World War II as the most economically and militarily powerful nation. After the war, the United States built up a global economic system, which enabled it to buy a network of military relationships—military alliances, bilateral military treaties, military interventions, military aid and so on. These military arrangements helped to support, often impose, sympathetic regimes and so provide a political framework for the capitalist economy and, also, the spread of the post-war technology paradigm.

The Soviet Union was, in the post World War II era, the only serious rival to the United States, and as a form of protection against Western economic and ideological expansionism, it too created a rival military network. The consequence was the bipolar division of the world which rested on the mutually dependent but antagonistic relationship between the United States and the Soviet Union, known as the Cold War. This Cold War was symbolised by the acquisition of ever more advanced weapons systems and consolidated by the permanence of a theoretical confrontation, by dramatising and extending an apparently perpetual imaginary war.

In both cases, it is probably true to say that institutions of the Cold War gave rise to an autonomous momentum for the arms race. In the US, large profit seeking armament corporations needed to develop ever more sophisticated forms of military technology in order to justify their continued profitable existence. In the Soviet Union, military and industrial institutions were structured to follow American initiatives even if those initiatives only made sense in the context of the imaginary war. But military technology absorbed considerable resources and extended as well as entrenched the postwar technology paradigm. This implied serious costs and these partly explain the relative economic decline of the United States and the Soviet Union in relation to other advanced industrial countries.

The consequence, in fact, has led to a divergence between the military dimension of the international system and the political, economic, and cultural dimensions. Because of the pervasive global nature of the Cold War, the dynamics of closing-in did not take an outright military form. The challenge of Europe and Japan, and later of the newly industrialising countries of the Third World, was primarily political and economic. Despite the fact that both the United States and the Soviet Union built up huge arsenals during the post-war period and both extended their military sway through their global military networks, the spheres of influence of both have gradually been eroded. For the Soviet Union, what seemed as the apparently monolithic post-war socialist world is now a divided house, starting with Yugoslavia's defection in 1948, then the Sino-Soviet split, the increasingly independent paths of North Vietnam and North Korea, as well as the restiveness and limited degrees of pluralism in Eastern Europe. The United States in the 1970s faced defeats in Indo-China, Southern Africa, Ethiopia, the Yemen and Iran, as well as the growing independence of Western Europe and Japan.

What is interesting is the way in which the relative decline of each superpower within its respective sphere of influence has continued to be perceived in military terms and interpreted by each as a zero-sum game in which the decline of one must mean the rise of the other. In the United States the decline is attributed to the Soviet military build-up, the fact that under the Nixon government the US was forced to accept 'parity' in the SALT agreements. For the Soviet Union, the problem is the Reagan Administration's quest for 'superiority'. Yet, surely, in a nuclear age, 'superiority' has no meaning as 'parity' is attained as soon as both sides possess nuclear weapons. In the event of an actual nuclear exchange, all that would matter is the 'parity' of human extinction. 'Parity' and 'superiority' only have meaning in terms of the imaginary war, fought out on the computers or in military exercises on both sides. Yet both the United States and the Soviet Union have a vested interest in continuing to believe in the imaginary war and, hence also, in the significance of the military dimension of global power. This fact, together with the autonomous pressure from military-industrial institutions, explains the continued momentum of militarisation. In what follows, we describe briefly how this affects the challengers —Europe, the Asia-Pacific region, and the Third World—in practice.

Europe is the most heavily militarised region in the world, at least as measured by military spending and numbers of weapons

Militarisation: The Imaginary War

and troops. Over two thirds of the American defence budget and 90 percent of the Soviet defence is estimated to be designed for a war in Europe. All three forms of structural determinants—autonomous military-industrial pressure, US and Soviet hegemony and the action-reaction of the East-West conflict—have combined in an escalating process of militarisation in Europe.

Since the late 1970s the East-West conflict has intensified and many of the gains made during the détente period have been eroded. This was primarily a consequence of growing fissures, on the one hand between Western Europe and the United States and, on the other hand, between the Soviet Union and Eastern Europe. It is important to realise that the Cold War period acted as a form of internal cohesion, holding nations together through fear of the 'enemy' and through the integration of the institutional structure of the State, or at least the military component thereof, in the alliance systems. Of course the two alliances were not identical. NATO, which was formed in 1949, was based on voluntary cooperation between the governments of the United States and the various countries of Western Europe. West European States voluntarily abrogated their sovereignty in giving the United States government the right to wage and direct a war in Europe. The American relationship to Western Europe may be described as 'hegemony' in that it was based on the consent of the West European States. This was much less true of the States of Southern Europe, especially Greece and Turkey; their relationship with the US can be better described as a relationship of domination. The Soviet relationship with Eastern Europe was more like the US relationship to Southern Europe; it depended to a much greater extent on actual or threatened physical presence, though there is no doubt at all that this was cemented by ideological cohesion that pervaded all these States. But whatever the motivations, the formation of the Warsaw Pact in 1955 provided a mechanism for integrating East European armed forces under Soviet command.

The period of détente weakened the cohesive role of the alliances and exposed differences, and even conflicts of interest. For Western Europe, these differences were primarily economic; they had to do with the use of the international economic system by the United

States to serve its own interests. Hence, there were disputes about interest rates, tariffs on food and steel, non-tariff barriers, etc. These spilled over into political conflicts about policy towards the Third World (where the United States and Western Europe have very different national interests) and about East-West relations. Europe had much more to gain from detente, in economic, political and cultural terms, than the United States.

In the context of America's economic decline *vis-a-vis* West Europe and Japan and its political decline worldwide in the aftermath of the Vietnam war, the only way in which American hegemony could be maintained and reasserted was in the military dimension. Hence the new emphasis on American military strength, particularly in nuclear weapons. Nuclear weapons had always symbolised the relationship of the United States with Europe. The United States was supposed to have provided a nuclear 'umbrella' for Western Europe because, apart from Britain and France, West European countries did not possess their own nuclear weapons.

This was the significance of the 1979 Double Track decision, in which NATO decided to go ahead with the deployment of Cruise and Pershing II missiles. The argument that this was a response to Soviet SS-20 missiles came later. At the time the decision was made, missiles were seen as a way of consolidating the political relationship between Europe and the United States by both European and American establishments. In this sense the missile deployment represented a re-emphasis on the coercive element of inter-State relationships.

The latest phase of the arms race in Western Europe is the US Army's adoption of the new 'AirLand Battle' doctrine and its attempt to gain NATO acceptance for the doctrine and the call by NATO's Supreme Commander for real increases in military spending by the European NATO countries. 'AirLand Battle' is a new offensive doctrine which puts great emphasis on striking deep into Warsaw Pact territory and on the integration of conventional, nuclear, chemical and electronic warfighting, making use of superior American technology. The concept of AirLand Battle would also be applied to 'out-of-area' or Third World situations. Alongside the proposals for AirLand Battle in Central Europe has come the build-up in the North Atlantic and the new emphasis on offensive naval operations, using launched cruise missiles—a maritime version of AirLand Battle.

Now, in explaining these trends, one should not underestimate the military-industrial pressure for escalation of the arms race. In the United States, despite the increases in the budget, expenditure is simply insufficient to guarantee full employment of industrial capacity, expanded as a result of advanced military technology. On the one hand, there is considerable pressure to increase the US expenditure on armaments. The story of the Cruise missiles is, in fact, very largely a story of military contractors seeking new outlets. On the other hand, there is considerable pressure to export arms. Since the early 1970s, American arms manufacturers have become much more dependent on exports, in some cases for their very survival. NATO by itself accounts for just over a quarter of total US arms exports.

In Western Europe, too, there is a strong autonomous pressure for rearmament. Some European leaders are calling for a more independent West European Defence policy. France and West Germany have proposed a revitalisation of the West European Union. Their ideas are in keeping with the pressure from the West European defence industry which has grown considerably over the last twenty years. The British and Swedish arms industries have always been substantial but now the French, Italian and West German arms industries are equally large and compete with the United States and the Soviet Union for world markets. These industries are heavily dependent on exports. They are also involved in many collaborative ventures like the Tornado multi-role combat aircraft developed and produced jointly by Britain, West Germany and Italy. This is because no single European country can afford to develop and produce modern weapons systems by itself. To secure the uncertain future of the European defence industry there is considerable pressure for increases in European purchases of conventional weapons and for greater European autonomy in arms procurement. These pressures have been reflected in the recent report to the European Parliament advocating a European arms procurement agency.

The Soviet military build-up in Europe continued steadily during the period of détente. There was an increase in nuclear weapons deployed in the western part, particularly the SS-20 medium-range missiles aimed at Western Europe. There was also an increase in and modernisation of conventional forces stationed in Eastern Europe. East European military budgets also increased except in Hungary and Poland. However, their military apparatuses have been increasingly integrated into the overall Warsaw Pact command system and a kind of military division of labour has been established both with respect to military tasks within the Warsaw Pact and as regards military aid to Third World countries. Military production in the countries of Eastern Europe (as distinct from military budgets) appears to have declined. Poland and Czechoslovakia used to produce advanced Soviet aircraft and tanks under licence but do so no longer. Bulgaria and East Germany produce electronic components for Soviet military equipment.

Undoubtedly this build-up and integration in the East was in part related to the military build-up in the West. For historic and political reasons, there exists among Soviet leaders and the Soviet people a deep-seated fear of invasion from the West. Nevertheless, NATO forces in Western Europe are not configured, at least not before the implementation of AirLand Battle, for offensive action. Moreover, it is difficult to understand why the Soviet Union has, in a nuclear age, sought 'parity' with the West. From time to time, there has been talk, especially during the Khruschev years, of adopting a minimum deterrent position and reducing conventional forces in Europe. But these ideas have never been adopted by the Soviet Union.

One reason is the ideological interest in sustaining internal coherence and integration within Eastern Europe in the face of the East-West conflict. Although it is true that the Soviet Union has advocated détente and peaceful co-existence, it is also the case that the 'threat' from the West justifies and legitimises the Soviet presence in Eastern Europe. The Soviet military doctrine, promulgated in 1962, which provided the premise for the subsequent Soviet military build-up, placed considerable emphasis on the integration of Warsaw Pact military forces. After 1968, the Soviet Union augmented its conventional forces in Eastern Europe and has made it clear in the Mutual Balanced Force Reduction (MBFR) talks in Vienna that

Militarisation: The Imaginary War

some of these should be counted as garrison troops.

It is probably true to say that during the period of détente, the role of the Western threat as a form of ideological coercion weakened and this may explain the role of new movements, such as Solidarnosoc in Poland. Just as Cruise and Pershing II missiles were designed to 'recouple' Western Europe and the United States, so the deployment of Soviet nuclear weapons in Eastern Europe, allegedly in response to the deployment of Cruise and Pershing II missiles, may be designed as a visible expression of the Soviet role in Eastern Europe. This is the first time the Soviet Union has publicly announced the deployment of Soviet nuclear weapons in Eastern Europe. There are also autonomous or autistic institutional pressures in the Soviet Union that should not be overlooked. But these operate differently than in the West. Pressures in the West for technological progress arise largely from the competitive nature of Western arms manufacturers. In the Soviet Union, by contrast, the pressures are rather those of bureaucratic rigidity. Those who received the largest share of the budget this and the last year are in a position to bargain for the largest share of the budget next year. The military-industrial sector has always occupied an important role in the Soviet economic system. There has always been an emphasis on quantity. Thus, large numbers of tanks are produced, in part, because this has always been the case. And then there is the need to accept ever new technologies requiring still more military spending. This largely comes as a reaction to greater sophistication in the West.

The Asia Pacific Region

In recent years, we have seen an eastward shift in global power relations. The Pacific appears to have become much more important in the military calculations of both the United States and the Soviet Union. As a result, the Cold War which originated in and over Europe has been reproduced in the Asia-Pacific region with a time-lag of one to a few years. So long as this region was not considered crucial to the Cold War, the direct military tension between the two superpowers was not so keen as in Europe. On the other hand, precisely because of its semi-peripheral character, the divided countries in this region—Korea and Vietnam—experienced deadly warfare which Germany, which was at the core, did not. Further, unlike Europe, there is virtually no neutral or neutralist country in this region. (The 'neutrality' espoused by ASEAN arouses many reservations.) Also, unlike Europe, the presence of a liberal parliamentary democracy and advanced industrial economy is confined to Japan alone. The result is that Japan has gradually dissociated itself from Third World Asia and turned itself into a 'member of the West', militarily dependent upon the United States. All these tendencies helped to perpetuate the Cold War in the Asia-Pacific region. Until recently the United States has held the position of overwhelming military superiority in this region. This, however, has provoked a rapid arms build-up by the Soviet Union which is considered to be approaching 'parity' in this theatre as well. Under the conditions of the sharp East-West conflict the two Koreas have been highly militarised, externally and internally. South Korea deploys as many as 400,000 men. North Korea allocates even more. And both regimes are highly authoritarian.

With its growing economic power, Japan has begun to play an increasingly active political and military role. In part, this has to be seen in terms of Japan's role as an outpost of world capitalism in East Asia, and in part in terms of the increasing conflicts of interest with the United States in the region. From the US perspective, the militarisation of Japan locks Japan more closely into the US-Japan relationship and constrains independent Japanese activity. There is also autonomous pressure from the US defence industry for increased exports to Japan, and in recent years, from the Japanese defence industry for relaxation of control over arms production and exports.

In contrast to the developments in Europe, the East-East conflict has been much more intense in the Asia-Pacific region, and has taken an openly antagonistic form. It began as the Sino-Soviet conflict which can largely be characterised as China's challenge to Soviet 'hegemonism'. This was greatly complicated by the conflict between China and Vietnam, and that between Vietnam and Kampuchea. These conflicts aggravated the militarisation of the socialist States in Asia and not just because of the loss of credibility of socialist ideology as a source of alternative vision of a peaceful, humane international order. The causes of these conflicts are complex. One can, for instance, point to the historical legacy of the States involved in these conflicts in that the idea of equality of nations did not exist in this region and instead a hierarchical order, or even a pecking order, prevailed between the Soviet Union, China, Vietnam and Kampuchea.

The Asia-Pacific region includes countries which have been pursuing a somewhat distinctive development paradigm for several decades. As we shall see in the next section, this paradigm contains its own internal dynamics of militarisation. This form of internal militarisation is best illustrated by the NICs (Newly Industrialising Countries) such as South and North Korea, Taiwan, Singapore, the Philippines and Indonesia. As a result of widening internal disparities and the emergence of technocratic oppressive regimes, large segments of the people have been marginalised and deprived, a condition which gives rise to the fear on the part of the privileged elite that 'communists' will instigate unrests. As in other Third World regions, internecine traditional conflicts between different ethnic and religious groups have been carried forward and have become more and more destructive and violent, for example, Malays versus Chinese in Malaysia, Burmese versus Karens and Shans in Burma, and Christians versus Moslems in the Philippines. This has in turn intensified the militarisation of the region and made it a part of the international security paradigm.

The Third World

If the power structure of the world were to be described in military terms, it would consist of two gigantic pyramids, headed by the military-industrial-bureaucratic complex of the United States and the Soviet Union, which dominate the militarily less advanced countries, particularly the Third World countries. The transfer of arms and military technology in various forms to local elites in Third World countries, along with the transfer of capital and technology, is one of the ways in which this hierarchical world order is sustained. Local elites acquire the capability for making war with such transfers and this strengthens their ideological and political role in their societies. But this structural dominance and disparity in the international hierarchy has got superimposed on the internal structure of repression, reinforcing both the international and the domestic order. This hierarchical military order has provided the framework within which Third World countries pursue 'development'.

The acquisition of modern weapons systems is clearly associated with certain forms of 'modernisation' and industrialisation based on the post-war technology paradigm. Arms transfers create a chain of supplementary demands for airfields, roads, telephones, radar systems, repair shops, special skills, manufacture of spare parts, especially special types of steel and petroleum products. It has been argued that these infrastructural demands, particularly where domestic arms manufacture is undertaken (as is the case with India, Egypt, and several Latin American countries), can represent the main impetus behind industrialisation, biassing industrialisation towards the types of industry which are characteristic of arms production in rich countries. In countries like Argentina and Brazil, for example, the construction of a diversified arms industry—shipbuilding, aerospace and armoured cars—with the assistance of foreign arms companies, especially Britain, France and West Germany, has played a central role in industrial development. Many commentators have noted the profound influence of arms imports and production on the formation of national research and development centres in heavy industries, as well as transport and communication.

Obviously this form of industrialisation is very expensive. It is highly capital-intensive, import-intensive, energy-intensive and skill-intensive. Arms imports average between one fifth and one half of the total capital imports of Third World countries. The investment required to create one job in the arms industry is much greater, especially in terms of foreign exchange than investment in civilian industry, or agriculture. Moreover, this job is likely to require the kind of skill that is scarce in underdeveloped countries. Also, the resulting gains in industrialisation or technological capabilities do not generate further resources. The evidence is unclear as to whether such industrialisation has any positive effect on growth. But apart from the rare examples of successful arms exports by Third World countries, the general truth is that they can never learn enough to compete with their arms suppliers in the world market for advanced technology products. And of course the technology is wholly inappropriate to solve some of the basic problems—hunger or disease—of Third World societies.

In order to pay for this type of military-industrialisation, the Third World countries must either obtain foreign assistance, through grants or loans, or they must increase the export of primary products obviously extracted from a poor economy. The consequent impoverishment of the countryside is well known. Rural producers have been drawn into the money economy (which results in a fictitious statistical increase in agricultural income) as more and more commodities are produced for urban and world markets instead of for the peasants' own subsistence. Cheap labour is drawn into towns as poor farmers and artisans are squeezed out by the introduction of more efficient capitalist methods of agriculture and production, by worsening terms of trade between manufactures and commodities, or by imports of cheap food from industrialised countries. Yet jobs are scarce in the towns because industrial investment is capital-intensive. The consequence is the characteristic pattern of grossly uneven development, extremes of wealth and poverty, within towns, between town and country, between regions and even between nations. All this has already produced immense social and cultural dislocation. It is a turbulent process, throwing up rural resistance, cultural conflict, urban riots, civil wars, international rivalries, and more. Moreover the recession in advanced industrial countries, with high interest rates, high food and oil prices and a fall in commodity prices, has greatly exacerbated the situation. A large number of people have been literally marginalised with nothing to produce and nothing on which to subsist. It is slow mass death without nuclear war.

It is this turbulent process that is 'crisis managed' by the international military order. The local elites through their linkage to the superpowers' militarisation become, as it were, the local agents of the global military order. During the 1960s, it was fashionable among Western sociologists to argue that Third World armies had become the spearhead of 'modernisation' or 'westernisation' or 'nation-building'. The Third World soldier or pilot who learns to use a modern weapon system becomes the Western industrial man.

He acquires familiarity with modern industrial and managerial techniques and a vested interest in an industrial environment in which modern military techniques can be utilised effectively. His role in the institutions of the State is strengthened. Through the military as well as other institutions, the development 'paradigm' permeates elite attitudes and legitimises internal repression, regional conflict as well as the ideological projection of internal and regional conflicts onto the Cold War. One must pay a 'price for progress', they say.

'Deterrence' or Cold War can be seen as a device for perpetuating the hegemonic position of the advanced States. But to the Third World peoples, at the bottom of both the pyramids, these ideological concerns seem remote. It is here that the conflicts are most intense and the 'management' process least effective. 'Deterrence' cannot prevent the actual outbreak of war. Extreme social and political tensions, combined with economic crisis, create the psychoses of war and oppression. They tempt aggressive adventures or mad acts of bravado. But then 'deterrence' can tolerate the peripheralisation of war. As long as war is confined to the lower levels of militarisation, to the bottom of the pyramids, it can be ignored and disregarded, however much suffering is involved.

But how long can violence be contained in the Third World? The process of superpower militarisation is nurtured both politically and economically by the global spread of militarisation. How long can the advanced industrial nations insulate themselves from the consequences?

Countervailing Pressures

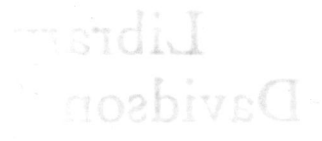

The people in the world, having suffered for long from militarisation, have now begun to react. Countervailing pressures have emerged, on the one hand, out of the growing divergence between the imaginary war in Europe and the experience of the actual war in the Third World and, on the other hand, out of the divergence between the military dimension of the global order and the political, economic, cultural and other dimensions. In Europe itself there is a profound loss of faith in what is known as 'deterrence'. To many people, World War III is no longer perceived as an exciting replay of the best parts of World War II: the struggle against fascism and so forth. Rather, it is increasingly viewed as a horrific extension of the worst parts—Hiroshima and Nagasaki, Hamburg, Dresden and Tokyo. The fear of war has become greater than the fear of the enemy. Every attempt by the United States and the Soviet Union to increase the 'credibility' of the imaginary war through the development of usable nuclear weapons or of 'nuclear equivalent' conventional weapons has merely served to spread fear and to initiate a search for alternatives to a perpetual Cold War.

Disaffection with 'deterrence' is not only European. Before the Vietnam war, the United States was able to use show of force to 'manage' Third World conflicts. Today the arsenals of the United States and the Soviet Union are not attributes of political power to the same degree. Despite the immense superiority, at least in terms of military technology, the United States was unable to 'win' in Vietnam. It was not able to 'win' in Iran either. The wars in Grenada and the Falklands have been mockeries of the imaginary war. Almost the entire British fleet was required to invade a small island with 1800 inhabitants, leaving the eastern Atlantic virtually defenceless, without a supposedly vital supply of the so-called spectrum of deterrence. Likewise, a very substantial American force was required to attack a tiny, poorly-defended island in the Caribbean, raising serious questions about the US ability to intervene in more dangerous situations in the world. Currently, the Soviet Union seems unable to establish its military superiority decisively against the *mujahideen* fighters of Afghanistan.

The loss of absolute belief in deterrence is not only a loss of belief in military power of the big nations. It also entails a questioning of the symbols and structures of militarisation transferred by them to the rest of the world. In actual wars, the aircraft and missiles and other instruments of modern technology often do not perform well; they turn out to be unreliable, create huge logistical problems and are unsuitable for countries which lack the appropriate infrastructure. Lorries carrying home-made bombs may achieve the same military goals as a much more sophisticated military artefact. To what extent, then, does the acquisition of modern military technology represent political power, either externally or domestically?

We have been witness to the fact that the various components of the imaginary war—the weapons, the military ideas, the relationship with the superpowers—no longer confer the same legitimacy to those governments which participate in the global military order. Militarisation may, or very often may not, enhance the capability to fight actual wars and, just as important, it may or may not enhance faith in the capability to fight actual wars. Hence, the political utility of show of force is also weakened.

It is this frustration with the self-deterring effects of nuclear weapons that has led to an increased emphasis on the possibility of fighting limited nuclear wars. Nuclear weapons are losing their political utility. When politicians worry about 'credibility', they are worrying about the psychological effectiveness of imaginary war. The concept of a limited nuclear war is supposed to increase 'credibility', to make actual war more plausible and so increase the political utility of nuclear weapons. Thus, there is real danger that the loss of belief in imaginary war could bring actual war closer.

The erosion of 'deterrence' does not just stem from the divergence between real and imagined wars. So long as the bipolar global order was successful in providing a framework for the two post-war paradigms, there existed a widespread common interest in accepting the 'story' about deterrence, which legitimised bipolarity. Today, there is a growing disinclination to accept this story.

Furthermore, militarisation is undermining many of the achievements of the post-war period. In both East and West heavy military spending seems to have been the major cause of the slowdown in economic growth experienced during the 1970s. In the West, military spending directly competes with welfare spending and in the East, military spending competes with resources available to raise living standards. More importantly, military technology, by both upholding and shaping the post-war technology paradigm, has inhibited technological alternatives and contributed to the decline of productivity growth. In the West continued militarisation is also weakening many hard-won democratic rights, and calling into question the working of representative democracy; this is a result of the way in which military decisions are hidden from public scrutiny and the way in which articulate opposition to military decisions is ignored. In the East, the sharpening of the East-West conflict and the escalation of the arms race has been accompanied by a tightening of domestic political discipline. Because the military burden is largely carried by the United States and the Soviet Union, militarisation has also increased the divergencies between these two States and the other advanced industrial countries. In the Third World, as we have seen, militarisation has distorted the development paradigm beyond recognition, accentuating political, social and economic inequality. Militarisation has also exposed the disbenefits of the post-war paradigm— resource extravagance, environmental destruction, cultural abuse and destabilisation of community lifestyles.

Nor is the process of militarisation itself immune from these new diseases of bipolarity. Within the armed forces, questions have been asked about the validity of military roles and the utility of military technology. The breakdown of military authority in the US Army in the Vietnam war was but one example of the fragility of military structures designed for the imaginary war, when tested in actual combat. Within the arms industry it has become clear that neither exports (which are unreliable) nor military spending can ever rise fast enough to ensure full employment of capacity.

Perhaps the most important of the countervailing pressures has been the growth of a mass movement for peace, especially in Europe and Australasia, but also in the United States and Japan. In some West European countries, e.g., Britain, Holland or West Germany, the peace movement is now much larger than the main political parties and is able to mobilise millions. In Denmark, New Zealand and Greece, the peace movement has brought about changes in government policy. These movements share the characteristics of new social movements. They have grown out of a disillusionment with party politics and a sense that the way to achieve change lies not in capturing State power but through changing ideas and accountability of the State to popular opinion. In Eastern Europe, small but not insignificant independent peace groups have emerged which oppose the Cold War and the militarisation of their own societies.

A growing disaffection with bipolarity is evident among sections of the elite too, especially in the militarily less advanced countries in Europe, Japan, Australasia and the Third World. There is a growing sense that bipolarity with its underlying belief in deterrence no longer serves as a form of political legitimacy. For many members of the establishment, civil servants, journalists and lawyers, militarisation actually appears to interfere with the very systems it is supposed to defend, whether we are talking about liberal democracy or socialism. And there are also those within the military-industrial complex who are concerned about their future: there are soldiers who lack experience of battle and are asking questions about defence policies, and there are defence workers who face the risk of unemployment and are beginning to at least think about the conversion of their industry for socially useful purposes.

Finally, there are the grassroot social movements of the Third World, movements of the landless and tribal peoples, women's movements, ecology movements and nationality movements, all of whom are challenging the sources of oppression in their societies. The opposition to State violence and to the militarisation of the State (as well as to artificially simulated threats from neighbours) is expressed by human rights movements or by movements like those against military rule in Latin America. All such movements need to be understood as the Third World counterparts of the peace movement in the advanced industrial societies. And they carry in them important components of a peace movement, defined in wholly indigenous, holistic terms.

These countervailing pressures could precipitate confrontation. The need to reassert the 'credibility' of the imaginary war or the significance of the bipolar global military order or just the need to satisfy the demands of the soldiers and defence workers could provide a new impetus to the 'hawks'. What is required is, therefore, a programme of demilitarisation that is sufficiently broad to encompass these countervailing pressures and yet sufficiently focussed to be applicable and achievable in particular situations, a programme that is sufficiently radical to be meaningful and sufficiently modest to avoid confrontation.

A Programme of Demilitarisation

Demilitarisation, according to our conception, must at the very least mean a lessening of physical coercion, both international and domestic. Simply put, internationally it entails dealignment; domestically it involves democratisation. But these are not conceived as the byproducts of demilitarisation; rather, demilitarisation is taken to be a process in which disarmament and the lowering of military tension, increased East-West and North-South exchange leading to greater diversity of international relationships, expanded space for new social, economic and cultural policies, and the run down of military-industrial complexes are all intertwined. Moreover, the process has to be a matter for popular responsibility. It must provide a sense of involvement among citizens in both East and West and North and South. It necessarily must come from outside the institutions of the Cold War, and it must be sufficiently extensive to prevent a militaristic backlash. A programme of demilitarisation can only be developed collectively by those directly involved in the struggle to achieve it. We can only suggest certain principles which, according to our analysis, ought to be respected.

Peace movements and social movements have to campaign for independent disarmament strategies. Independent acts of disarmament are often called 'unilateral' acts. The purpose of an unilateral act is often seen as a way of breaking the deadlock in multi-lateral negotiations. It is criticised by those who support multilateral negotiations on the ground that it could create 'imbalance'. But the purpose of an 'independent' act of disarmament is also to move away from the notion of 'sides' and 'balances'; it is an act of political abstention from the idea of deterrence. It is worth reiterating that a true military balance is a war which no one wins. When politicians talk about a military balance they are talking about the political *status quo* which is based on beliefs about the imaginary war. In reality, no one would win a nuclear war; so numbers are meaningless. They have a meaning only in terms of the imaginary war where nuclear weapons are not supposed to destroy everything. Since we reject the current version of an imaginary war, we also reject current notions of 'balance'. A political abstention from the idea of deterrence is also an assertion of political responsibility: that disarmament is too important a matter to be left to those who have the dubious privilege of participation at the negotiating table. The demand for a nuclear-free Europe, for example, is a way of refusing, in principle, the present military order.

These independent acts of disarmament need to be tailored to each individual, local or national, situation. At a tactical level they can involve the demand for nuclear-free zones, municipal, national or regional. They can involve opposition to weapon systems like the Cruise and Pershing II missiles or to nuclear warfighting strategies as implied by the campaigns for 'No First Use' or against civil defence programmes. Yet, at the same time, the campaigns for independent acts of disarmament have to be organised cooperatively with grassroot movements. The campaign against Cruise and Pershing II missiles has proved to be an extraordinary example of grassroot cooperation in Western Europe and the United States. Such a combination of independence and cooperation is required not only to counter the strength of the concept of deterrence but also, through our own practice, to create and spread alternative ideas and institutions.

Ideally, it ought to be possible to develop a global set of principles which can be applied independently. One such proposal would combine the demand for a freeze on the development and production of all nuclear weapons with the demand for the withdrawal of all nuclear weapons deployed on foreign territory or on foreign territorial waters. Such a proposal would simultaneously aim to halt the arms race and eliminate coercion in the relations between nuclear and non-nuclear States. It would mean the withdrawal of Soviet and American nuclear weapons from Europe as well as from some Third World countries; it would also prohibit visits of naval vessels carrying nuclear weapons to non-nuclear States, or the application of East-West war fighting practices to the Third World as in the case of the US Rapid Deployment Force. It would halt the further acquisition of nuclear weapons by the United States, the Soviet Union, Britain, France and China. As a global initiative, the proposal would demonstrate the solidarity and the cooperation of peace movements and sympathetic non-aligned States. As a domestic initiative, the proposal can be translated into national demands which can be independently pressed upon governments.

Independent acts of disarmament would have to be accompanied by proposals for alternative defence policies, both for nations and for military alliances, for advanced industrial countries and for Third

World countries. These policies must come to terms with the existing reality of East-West conflict and the actual danger of war and at the same time make possible an alternative reality in which war has receded.

There has been a good deal of discussion at least as regards advanced industrialised countries, about the way in which alternative *defensive* or non-provocative non-nuclear defence postures might satisfy this requirement. Such proposals might be promoted with NATO by the smaller countries, viz., Norway, Denmark, Holland and Belgium as well as Britain. Ideas about alternative defence policies can also be drawn up with respect to Third World countries, especially the possibilities for reducing their reliance on excessively expensive and sophisticated foreign military technology. This is, in fact, a way in which Third World countries can put pressure on advanced industrial nations; the refusal to pay for the surplus military industrial capacity of the industrial nations is a potentially powerful lever.

Disarmament and alternative defence policies, however, make sense only within the context of a strategy for overcoming or eroding the present bipolar military order. What is clearly of first importance is that we establish a new form and content in international dialogue, especially between East and West. Already, Western peace movements and professional groups like doctors and scientists have taken a lead in establishing new forms of informal dialogue across the East-West divide. Greater understanding of each other's situation is one of the best ways to expose the Cold War ideology. This form of a dialogue should also be followed and extended by trade unions, women's groups and so on. Moreover, the same principle ought to apply to North-South discourse. We need a mechanism in which a concrete rather than theoretical connection can be established between those in need and those who waste resources on armaments.

International and national approaches to disarmament and dialogue require, perhaps specially in the West, a change in the *institutions* of deterrence, in particular the military-industrial complex. The conversion of the arms industry to socially useful production has to be seen not as something which follows disarmament, but a preparation for disarmament, a way of mobilising interest around alternatives to the arms race, and to the ongoing process of demilitarisation. Thus, conversion, for instance, has to be able to develop an alternative institutional framework that combines stability, especially for employment that is guaranteed by the State, with dynamic possibilities for innovation. One could, for example, envisage an international agency which brought trade unions in the armament industry together with those in the Third World who need their kind of industrial skills, with resources sufficient to carry out specified concrete projects. Local and national agencies could also be established which could back groups of workers and/or local communities who wish to prepare plans for conversion and apply for funds to carry out such plans.

Perhaps the common denominator of these suggestions is that they cannot be inserted into government policies or decided on by a fiat, and that is perhaps how they differ from or go beyond the measures that make up current arms control policy. Rather, they have to be insisted and imposed on governments by persistent and outspoken groups of interest and they have to be capable of extending those groups and mobilising new groups. Demands for independent measures of disarmament and alternative defence policies, for international dialogue have to provide new forms of local, national and regional political participation. Already, new political changes are occurring within the framework of demands for disarmament. The declaration of municipal nuclear-free zones in Europe represents an assertion of local political responsibility. Similarly, there are demands for increased accountability to Parliament. New debates have also emerged about secrecy, the role of the media, and the political position of women who have played a leading role in many peace movements. Only some such ongoing process, which has to be part of a strategy for dealignment and democratisation as well as demilitarisation, can provide an alternative to deterrence and bipolarity.

This political process has to be international and global. The strategy for demilitarisation has to be developed and campaigned for through continuous interchange across national boundaries, through greater understanding of other political situations and perspectives. In this way, a changing political process, both domestic

Militarisation: The Imaginary War

and international, actually creates the space for the policies of global transformation. In effect, it involves the transformation of the nation-State. And of thinking about security.

3

The World Economic Crisis

From some perspectives, we have been witnessing over the last thirty years a permanent state of crisis. There has been a worsening impoverishment of millions of people in the Third World, the degradation and depletion of the environment, violence and bloodshed and abuses of human dignity and freedom in many places.

The economic crisis which is being talked about so much emerged in late 1970s and early 1980s. It is characterised by the reappearance of mass unemployment in the industrialised countries of the West, the novel combination of inflation and stagnation known as stagflation, and by a disturbing expansion of international indebtedness. In fact, the economic crisis can be described as a crisis of material accumulation and not a crisis of byproducts; it is a crisis of industrial enclaves and of privileged consumerism; a crisis characterised by economic stagnation and the reversal of economic growth. All this arises largely from the unwillingness of the privileged to share the surpluses generated in earlier decades. There is a clear reluctance to undertake major structural changes in the economic and technological order and, consequently, to effect a slow-down of what is considered to be technological progress.

We realise that we need to be careful in using the term 'crisis'. In saying that it is a world crisis, we must cover all the major regions of the world, North, South, capitalist and socialist, and devise appropriate indicators for each region. We must also be clear about whether a crisis exists for all the socialist countries, or whether it does, in fact, exist for all the capitalist countries. For example, it is disputable whether Japan and Switzerland are in a crisis situation. It may also be the case that whilst the international institutions established to facilitate international trade and exchange are not able to cope with new challenges, these problems do not necessarily reflect a structural crisis but rather a problem of adjustment. We argue elsewhere in this essay that international capitalism is moving into a new cycle or a new technology paradigm (and dragging along with it, the socialist economies and those of the Third World, too,) marked by a rapid relocation of capital in areas such as electronics, automation, a new international division of skilled labour, etc. We have often been told that this new paradigm is going to be successful in displacing the older paradigms, despite painful consequences to the well-established beneficiaries of the earlier paradigms, e.g., countries such as Britain, or workers engaged in heavy industry. If this view has any validity, it would cast a different light on the situation. Are we then correct in describing the present economic problems as adding up to a 'crisis'?

Since conventional economic theories have largely failed to reveal the objective laws of motion of the world economy as an organism, or even to consider it as such, it is hardly surprising that even within the same school of thought we cannot find a consensus on whether the international economy has been suffering from a lasting crisis since the early seventies, or whether it has undergone some cyclical recessions and recoveries, perhaps twice since then, and whether the crisis, if any, originates in the economies of just a few countries. There are also widely differing assessments of the role of different types of economic and non-economic activities in the deterioration of international economic conditions, e.g., of monetary, financial, trade and price policies, protectionism and various forms of economic nationalism, of transnational corporations and cartel-policies, of demographic and ecological factors, of the armament dynamics and inter-State conflicts and so on.

The term 'crisis' itself has various interpretations. For some, it is a kind of catastrophe extending over a long historical period and threatening the collapse of the whole system. For others, it is only a cyclical phenomenon, a down-swing which is required to resolve temporarily the most acute contradictions and imbalances which have arisen; such a crisis would pave the way for a further upswing to be followed, perhaps, by a further crisis. And for yet some others, it is a culmination of conflicts and contradictions which may well lead to either a fascist military 'solution' or its exact opposite, i.e., a new 'social contract' and democratisation.

Characteristics of the Crisis

Without going into any kind of etymological discussion on the meaning of the term we can, on the basis of empirical studies, make the following five observations, which are, of course, interrelated.

1. In contrast to the earlier cases of cyclical recessions and recoveries, such typical symptoms of economic crises as high levels of unemployment, the presence of underutilised capacities and a dwindling rate of growth in the developed market economies have, since the early seventies, persisted and have actually survived the relative recovery of 1976-78.

2. In previous periods, depressions or periods of stagnation tended to be accompanied by a fall in prices, while recoveries and upswings were associated with rising prices. In contrast, since the early seventies the economy of most countries, particularly the developed market economies, has been characterised by a curious combination of stagnation and a high rate of inflation which appears as a new symptom of crisis or the symptom of a new kind of crisis.

3. In the past the economic crisis affected individual countries or certain groups of countries; if an international crisis developed, such as that of 1929-30, its epicentre could easily be identified and its spread was traceable. Since the early seventies, virtually all countries have, in various ways and degrees, been affected by a deterioration of economic conditions.

4. Although, in the past, too, the causes and effects of economic crises could not be wholly identified within the realm of purely economic phenomena, the present crisis is truly of a multidimensional nature. The obvious interlinkages and interactions of widely different processes and factors of world development which have informed the eruption or perpetuation of this crisis are unprecedented. We are witnessing the simultaneous appearance of the symptoms

of crisis, imbalances or deadlocks, not only in economic life but in energy supply, natural resource management, science and technology, the ecological system, population and nutrition, consumption patterns, life-styles, cultures, and in political institutions and ideologies as well.

5. Finally, the overall deterioration of the world economic conditions has occurred at a time when the threat to the very survival of humankind has also reached unprecedented proportions. It stems from the growth of the destructive capacities of modern armaments, induced by the international arms race, and from the desperate situation of millions of human beings suffering misery, hunger and sickness. Unlike the great crisis of 1920-30 which was followed rather than preceded by militarisation, today the arms race has actually preceded and continues to accompany economic crisis; this suggests that it has played a role in causing the crisis.

Background to the Crisis

We are still not ready to say that the sickness of the contemporary world economy is a global crisis. That diagnosis, as in medical praxis, would need a kind of *anamnesis*. We know that the basic inequalities and imbalances in the world economic system are deeply rooted in history but we need carefully to examine the post-World War II period of world development to identify the events and processes which actually prepared the way for the eruption of the sickness of the world economy as well as the reasons why it remained relatively latent for a while.

World War II was followed by a relatively long period of boom in the developed market economies and a rapid expansion of international trade. Though the American economy suffered a few minor recessions, the other developed market economies did not experience any serious crisis until the seventies, thanks to various (partly temporary) factors and conditions. These included the reconstruction of war-damaged economies; the effect of deferred demand for consumer goods in the former war economies; the spread of post-war technological and scientific revolution, inducing masssive investment waves and radical shifts in production and consumption structures; the start of economic integration in Western Europe; the opening of formerly closed imperial markets to capital and the rivalry accelerated internationalisation of capital investments; the forging ahead of transnational corporations, many of them based in the United States; the expansion of public expenditures and guaranteed markets; the rise of a 'consumer society' and the inflated credit system; the application of anti-cyclical government policies and the desynchronisation of the business cycles of the individual countries (at least temporarily). These conditions and factors—though some of them also contained the seeds of the coming crisis—concealed for some years certain basic contradictions in post-war economic development.

One such contradiction was the heavy reliance of the post-war international trade and monetary system on the economic leadership of the United States, with its strong dollar, large credit capacities, increased capital mobility, high level research and development (R&D) facilities, increasing competitive exports of high quality, technologically sophisticated industrial products and many other 'dynamic' factors. But all this was soon challenged by the other industrial powers and indeed by the process of transnationalisation itself. It was also further undermined by heavy military expenditures and the technological bias of the American economy.

The centrally planned economies of the socialist countries were rather isolated from the rest of the world in the period from the late forties to the mid-sixties, during the Cold War and because of it. In the first part of this period, the socialist countries carried out a successful but too rapid artificially accelerated and extensive-type of self-reliant industrialisation. This was achieved through restricting the rise of personal consumption and imposing a heavy burden on agriculture. Because of its more or less autarchic features resulting in duplication of effort, the process of industrialisation in socialist countries created certain obstacles to future specialisation not only in the worldwide division of labour but also within the Council for Mutual Economic Assistance (CMEA). In the second part of this period, a shift took place in economic policy in favour of a more balanced growth, increasing the living standards and devoting more attention to agriculture and consumer goods production, as well as the creation of a more organic, structurally complementary division of labour within the CMEA.

But this gave a new impetus to economic development, primarily in a sociological sense rather than in the sense of an artificially high accumulation rate as before, and this helped to keep the rate of economic growth of these countries at a high level. During the whole of the Cold War period, their rates of growth far exceeded the average rates of economic growth of the developed market economies as well as those of the Third World countries. Such high rates seemed to remain a more or less permanent feature of these economies even in the late 1960s and early 1970s, when as a result of détente, the East-West economic relations began to be normalised. This was also the time when trade relations between the socialist countries of Eastern Europe and a number of Third World countries began to expand.

With all this came the need for a change-over from the 'extensive stage' of economic development to an 'intensive stage' in the socialist countries. This transition was explained in terms of exhaustion of manpower resources required for extensive development rather than in terms of the consequences of integration of these countries into the world economy. Certain temporary difficulties and a slow-down in economic growth were expected to follow from such a change-over but all that was to be easily overcome by a further identification of cooperation in the context of the CMEA. Thus even after the crisis had erupted in the Western economies and the international markets, it was still assumed for years by many of the leading economists in the socialist countries that the crisis and its consequences (often attributed merely to a deterioration in terms of trade) would only slightly affect the centrally planned economies and the latter would be able to maintain their rate of growth, internal stability and equilibrium.

These economists failed to foresee the result of expanding contacts with the capitalist West, through tourism and communication. They did not anticipate the impact of the demonstration effects of the Western 'consumer society' on the pattern of consumer demand in their economically less affluent societies with a far narrower income differentiation than in the former. But in reality, a sudden demand explosion such as for automobiles, electric appliances and other consumer durables presented itself and it caused bottlenecks, imbalances and tensions. In most cases, economic policy reacted to the new problems and challenges with a certain delay and in new ways, e.g., by resorting to foreign loans. These turned out to be an unjustified charge both on the international liquidity situation of the future, and on their own debt servicing capacities.

The increasing economic difficulties of most of the developing countries of the Third World, particularly the low-income primary producing countries with high population growth, were already marked enough in the mid-fifties. However, these difficulties were hardly considered to be symptoms and warning signs of a deep and aggravating sickness in the world economy as a whole. This was because the rapid growth of international trade masked the linkage. That growth had been due primarily to the expansion of trade between the developed market economies. It gained momentum initially from the vitality of the US economy, then from the activities of transnational corporations, and subsequently from the reconstruction and integration of the economies of Western Europe and Japan within the framework of Welfare State policies, full employment, increasing wages and growing effective demand. All this, taken together with the high growth rates in Eastern Europe, suggested that the only 'sick man' of the world economy was the South, whose underdevelopment could easily be overcome. The pro-Western economists prescribed increasing the ties with the West from where capital, technology, skill, management etc., would be acquired. The pro-socialist economists recommend the opposite, i.e., delinking of the economy from the world market and emulating the industrialisation model of the East European socialist countries. A few developing countries in Latin America and South-East Asia followed the former course. They adjusted to the new business policy of the transnational corporations, got the transfer of certain industrial activities from the developed market economies to their countries and consequently, in a relatively short period, achieved a spectacular growth in manufacturing production. Certain other developing countries in West and East Africa chose a socialist path and also demonstrated a promising start in structural changes, self-reliance and income gap reduction. Both kinds of experience succeeded in reinforcing the assumptions of the economists in the prosperous North that the sickness of the world economic organism was only a symptom of the sick part.

The 'Germs' of Crisis

The period from World War II to the late 1960s already contained not only the 'germs' of the crisis but also some early symptoms and manifestations of it. It was this period when, paradoxically enough, despite vigorous growth of the world economy and expanding world trade, some of the basic contradictions inherent in the prevailing world economic system deepened. Along with the relatively undisturbed operation of the world market, widening gaps, disproportions and imbalances began to surface, and new discrepancies and anomalies developed on the global scene, all of which demanded a global solution and a new order.

Without providing a full list and going into details we want to highlight a few of the above contradictions, imbalances or discrepancies as they relate to the *problematique* of peace with transformation.

1. First of all, the centuries old colonial pattern of the international division of labour between the industrial metropolitan countries and their peripheries producing primary resources faced an operational crisis. This was manifested already in the mid-fifties in the rapidly declining share of the peripheral countries in world exports, in the dramatic deterioration in their terms of trade, in their cumulative indebtedness and in the very fact that extraordinary means and measures such as aid and military intervention became necessary to keep the system in operation. This had come about partly because of the positive changes in the political power structures, partly due to the shifts in production structures concomitant with a fast changing framework of science and technology, and also partly because of built-in imbalances.

As a consequence, a series of interlocking vicious circles appeared in international economic relations, particularly in relation to the primary resource producing countries of the Third World. To change their biased production structure and one-sided specialisation on primary products, they badly needed investment funds for which the main local source of finance was the export-oriented primary production. To compensate for losses from deteriorating terms of trade they increased the volume of primary exports, bringing a further decrease in relative prices. To keep their import purchasing power on a required level they had to resort to foreign loans, thereby devoting an increasing part of their future export revenues to debt servicing. To avoid or ease the severe indebtedness they tried to acquire external financial resources by attracting foreign direct investments which, however, also utilised scarce local resources and resulted in a regular outflow of investment incomes, so that the growth of foreign assets in the economy became a form of additional, disguised indebtedness. Finally, to meet the growing demand for food, stemming partly from the population explosion and partly because of the distorted structure of agricultural production biased for export, they had to resort to food imports. Once again, the payments for these reinforced the pressure to expand primary production for export, and this led to a further reduction in the capacity to produce food for domestic consumption, thereby aggravating the reliance on food imports. Such vicious circles have primarily affected those Third World developing countries which have remained within or deepened further the colonial pattern of specialisation in primary products.

The shifts in industrial structures and consumption patterns of the developed market economies combined with technological change have had a differential impact on the market position of various primary products. The post-war technology paradigm increased the demand for a few primary products such as crude oil and some strategic materials. But most primary products, particularly those which were substituted by synthetics, faced a declining rate of growth of demand. As a result, the terms of trade for almost all the primary producing developing countries showed a negative trend. The artificially depressed price level (the 'posted price' system) of crude oil, despite the expansion of demand, allowed only a marginally better position for the oil exporters. However, the tension between expanding oil consumption and low prices could not be suppressed indefinitely, particularly since oil exporters got politicised following the growing Arab-Israel cleavage and formed their own producers' association.

As we have observed earlier, some newly industrialised countries of the Third World, mainly in Latin America and Southeast Asia, geared their economy towards the requirements of transnational corporations by ensuring a hospitable investment climate, various allowances and 'free trade zones' or putting-out activities for industrial subsidiaries. In the process, they tied their economic development so much to the growth of Western economies, to Western technology and markets, that they became extremely vulnerable to a recession in the West. Such a policy of industrialisation, in both its import-substitutive and its export-oriented versions, was often built upon a contradiction between economic liberalism i.e., an 'open door' policy *vis-a-vis* the foreign companies, and political oppression especially against the working classes. The import-substitutive variant of this new industrialisation policy lost its momentum even before the world recession came; this was mainly because of its self-defeating character. For one thing, the product choice was biased by the consumer-orientation of the elites. For another, sophisticated technologies had to be imported, despite the narrow limits of the domestic market for luxury goods. All this inevitably led to balance-of-payments problems and indebtedness.

The changeover to export orientation promised better results so long as the world market also promised to keep on expanding. With their low-wage-cost products, the newly industrialising countries increasingly challenged many of the traditional industries of the West, thereby bringing the problem of structural adjustment to the fore and inducing some trade unions in the West to call for protection. At the same time, keeping the local wage level depressed and the labour movement oppressed led to the marginalisation of a large part of the rural sector of the population. The export-oriented countries have thus actually generated a socio-political tension in their societies and an economic imbalance in their development model which together have put the rural poor to an immense disadvantage in their struggle for survival.

2. The second set of factors has to do with the realm of global institutions. An international structure of economic institutions with 'rules of the game' was established at the end of the War (the Bretton

Woods monetary system, IMF, the World Bank, GATT, etc.) reflecting the primary concerns and interests of the major actors and the economic power relations prevailing at the time. This, however, came into conflict with the subsequent shifts in power relations, in particular the decline of American economic hegemony and the rise of Western Europe and Japan with new or newly articulated needs of the international community. The new structure inevitably affected the vital interests of the developing countries. Long before the eruption of the crisis of the 1970s, it became necessary to revise, reformulate or complement some of the established rules.

The post-war (Bretton Woods) monetary system was predicated on a reserve-currency exchange standard, centred on the US dollar with its convertibility into gold and accompanied by fixed exchange rates. In short, it was based upon the dominant position of the US economy in the world. Immediately after World War II, the 'dollar-hunger' of the war-damaged economies of Western Europe reinforced the world position of the US dollar. But later on, the US economy lost its vitality, partly because of the increasing outflow of US private investment to the European Common Market to enjoy internal positions there, and also to the low-wage developing countries. But the main reason, as we mentioned in the previous chapter, was the paralysing effects of the rigidities introduced into the US industrial structure by its commitment to a particular technology paradigm. The technology paradigm was manifested, above all, in the process of militarisation, in the continuous improvement of the weapons systems which alienated technology from new civilian requirements and in growing military expenditures which increasingly diverted investment, skilled personnel and R&D from civilian purposes. The relocation of industries by the US-based transnational corporations as well as rapid catching up by Western Europe and Japan with their relatively lower wage-costs and higher productivity growth brought about a sharpening competition between the US and other industrial countries. The worsening trade position of the United States, along with its on-going foreign expenditures on military bases, wars, tourism, aid, etc. increasingly weakened the US dollar, the very basis of the world monetary system. The subsequent abandonment of convertibility and of the introduction of fixed exchange rates was partly a consequence and partly an aggravating factor of the world economic crisis. All this has clearly revealed the contradiction of an international monetary system built upon a single national currency.

The international trade system, the General Agreement on Trade and Tariffs (GATT), established after World War II, was aimed primarily at the generalisation of bilateral trade concessions and the reduction of tariff barriers through the application of the most-favoured-nation principle. As such, it met the requirement of developed market economies to expand their trade relations initially between themselves and in traditional fields of trade. Neither the situation of the structurally weak underdeveloped countries nor that of the centrally planned economies was considered by the framers of GATT. Nor was the system able to cope with the rapidly unfolding trade in other fields such as skills, technology and services which had come in the wake of the phenomenal growth of the transnational corporations. These new phenomena and contradictions as well as the increasing role of non-tariff barriers, restrictive business policies and the rise of regional and sub-regional common markets, increasingly undermined the basic assumptions on which the trade system was built. Moreover, like Bretton Woods, the success of GATT also depended on the predominant trade position of the United States. As long as the United States enjoyed a current account surplus, or even large currency reserves, it could guarantee a liberal world economy through aid and loans as well as through various forms of political and military intervention. The decline in American economic and political power made this much more difficult. Indeed, things have now come to such a pass that the US itself violates the principles of free trade through tariffs, non-tariff barriers, the demand for voluntary restrictions on exports, high interest rates and so on.

3. Beyond the structural shifts in the world economy and the crisis in global institutions lie the constraints of the post-War technology paradigm. In theory, the post-war revolutions in science and technology opened up new sources of economic and social development and provided opportunities to solve many of the grave problems facing humankind. In reality, technological change, or the

application of science, was largely shaped by the economic and social structure of the advanced industrial countries, particularly the United States. Thus, forty per cent of the global military research and development expenditure came to be devoted to military purposes, as a result of the arms trade and the unfolding international arms race. Moreover, the application of scientific and technological resources of the civilian sector was biased toward elite demands which were energy intensive and inappropriate for the needs of the peoples in developing countries.

The potential for this kind of technological change was ultimately limited. As we have already noted, military technology became increasingly sophisticated and increasingly remote from civilian requirements so that the benefits of 'spin-off' declined. In addition, the rise of guaranteed (State) or oligopolistic (Transnational Corporations) markets, combined with the bureaucratisation of large enterprises and laboratories, constrained the impulse for innovation. In the military field, new generations of weapon systems were characterised by increasing costs for diminishing improvements in performance while in the civilian sector, productivity growth markedly declined. Perhaps because the post-war technology paradigm was first established in the United States, productivity growth in that country consistently lagged behind the productivity growth in Western Europe and Japan. From the late 1960s began the period of decline. With it also came the decline in the competitiveness of American exports which played an important role in undermining the post-war economic system.

The new technologies of the 1970s and the 1980s, microelectronics and biotechnology, have been diffused much more rapidly in Western Europe and Japan where the post-war technology paradigm was less rigidly-entrenched. However, the prevailing bias of intensive militarisation and elite consumerism, largely based on automotive and oil industries, and still dominated by the United States, calls into question how far these developments in Western Europe can offset the declining trend in productivity growth. Such a trend was also experienced by the centrally planned economies, despite the efforts to change over from an 'extensive' to an 'intensive' mode of accumulation.

4. The consumerism built into the post-war technology paradigm has had far-reaching consequences for the mass of the people everywhere. Most developed market economies produced a 'consumer society' in the post-war period. It was characterised by increasing real wages, expanding welfare measures and consumerism. But consumer society was partly, if not wholly, based upon the 'old' terms of international economic relations in which countries of the Third World supplied cheap energy and raw material resources. Hence, the national interests of these countries and their collective endeavours to achieve more remunerative prices for their products necessarily threatened the very foundations of the consumer society in the West.

Meanwhile, in the West itself class tensions were on the increase. The positive changes in income distribution and the new kind of 'social contract' achieved by the working classes and manifested in social welfare measures and the Keynesian economic interventions of the State created increased wage-costs and tax-burdens to the entrepreneurs. For a while, these burdens were offset by expanding market opportunities and productivity growth. However, by the late 1960s, the increasing self-confidence of the workers and consumers and their growing demands as expressed, for example, in the incidents of May 1968 in France or the Italian 'hot autumn' of 1969 began to threaten business interests, the competitiveness of exports and also the 'normal' accumulation of capital, since the temporary sources of the boom period had been exhausted. Moreover, the rising trend in real wages as well as in government expenditures on defence and social welfare was not accompanied by an appropriate productivity increase. This led to an imbalance between the rate of personal consumption and the rate of productive accumulation. The reaction of the private companies, particularly of the transnational corporations, to this development was to resort to price increases. This, along with government budget policy and deficit financing measures, accelerated the inflation process. These companies also resorted to the transfer of some industrial activities to less developed, low-wage countries. Both measures, however, undermined full employment which was an important pillar of the new 'socialist contract' in the developed market economies.

The international spread and demonstration effect of wasteful consumerism and 'Western' life-styles has finally reached the elite of many developing countries, including the poorest ones. This has not only sharpened domestic social inequalities and aggravated the position of the poorest people. It has increased the import needs and export dependence, and paved the way for a distorted form of industrialisation based on import-substitution of luxury consumer goods. And in some cases, import-substitution has meant military equipment produced with imported technology, often by transnational subsidiaries, involving very little local labour.

The run-away consumerism, the business-dictated fashion waves, the spread of private motorisation, as well as over-urbanisation and an excessive mechanisation and chemicalisation of agriculture have together brought about increasing danger of ecological disequilibrium, of depleting, by over-exploitation, some of the non-renewable natural resources, and of destroying, by pollution, the human environment. These trends, coupled with the demographic explosion and the over-specialisation of agriculture, have led to grave food shortages and the nutritional crisis of the 1980s and beyond.

5. Added to all this is the all-pervading role of transnational actors in the economies of all regions. Since World War II, transnational corporations have played an increasingly important role in developed market economies. But since the early 1960s, the relatively more developed countries of the Third World have also been penetrated by these corporations. Ironically, the New International Economic Order, which appeared as a demand of Third World governments in economic forums, turned out in reality to be a response to the needs of the country-based transnational corporations with headquarters in the advanced industrial countries. This was one of the main reasons why they took to industrial redeployment; it was not, as is sometimes thought, a consequence of import substitution policies adopted by the Third World countries.

Transnationalisation of the economies has aggravated all the problems of the Third World countries. The transnational corporations have not only established themselves principally in the so-called high technology industries but actually in the sectors producing intermediate goods as well as durable goods. The technology is designed for large markets but the domestic market tends to be much too narrow. Consequently, the industrialisation process brought in by the transnational corporations is characterised by unused capacity, high prices and weak productivity growth. Moreover, since these industries are geared towards a capitalist market and towards the high-income sector, it becomes necessary to strengthen the control of these firms over the local economy and to increase the income of the most privileged groups, since these have the highest propensity to consume the products of factories established by the transnational corporations. Such income concentration exacerbates the tendency to transplant consumerism to the poor countries of the Third World.

The transnational corporations have also increased the tendency towards agricultural exports, to the detriment of food production in Third World countries. This has led to both a scarcity of food which hits the mass of the already impoverished population and simultaneously to an increase in the import of food for basic dietary consumption. In some cases, e.g., Venezuela, food imports now account for as much as sixty per cent of national consumption. And such large food imports, in their turn, aggravate the balance of payments.

The deterioration of traditional agriculture stimulates rural-urban migration. We see this happening on a very large scale today throughout the Third World. But capital-intensive industrialisation favoured by the transnational corporations—and, of course, the Third World elites—cannot keep up with the growth of urban populations. The consequence is high levels of urban unemployment, marginalisation of the poor, personal insecurity for all, degradation of social services and other conditions of everyday life.

Finally, the transnationalisation process tends to transfer those industries from the advanced industrial centres which are heavy consumers of energy and destructive of the environment; pollution in developed countries is reduced by exporting polluting industries. Worse still, such industries compromise the future possibilities of self-sufficient and self-determined growth in the developing countries. Their economies, thereby, become even more dependent on foreign investment and foreign markets.

In both developed and developing countries, the transnational corporations have undermined State control of the economies. An increasing amount of international trade is 'internalised' as transfers between the subsidiaries operating in different countries; such trade is largely exempted from national control and the normal market mechanisms. Capital transfers are equally difficult to regulate and corporations can easily find mechanisms for evading taxation or foreign-exchange restrictions. Consequently, State interventions and anti-cyclical government policies become that much less effective. The trend towards regional integration and the promotion of common markets in Europe and South America has also weakened the economic power of national governments.

Transnationalisation has come into conflict with endeavours of many developing countries to achieve national integration and to build a real national economy. Several developing countries, having woken up to this fact, have launched an attack on foreign capital which occupies the commanding heights of their economies. Some have nationalised foreign firms and proclaimed a policy of self-reliance. But, in quite a few cases, subsequent counter-attacks, retaliatory measures, credit freezes, the withdrawal of aid or imposition of trade bans by the affected industrial countries have created insurmountable difficulties for developing countries. Extreme retaliatory measures have taken the form of *coups d'etat*. But even ordinary counter-measures have often led to resource and skill scarcities, weaknesses and distortion in the local economy. Some Third World countries, therefore, have been forced to shift or modify their economic policy, once again providing openings for foreign capital and economic relations with the North. In short, transnationalisation has come into conflict with State sovereignty in both the North and the South.

6. The last set of factors relates to the interrelation of the economic crisis with the phenomena of war and repression. The growing discrepancy between developments in the world economy and the global State structure is a major reason for increasing domestic and inter-State conflicts, violence and wars. As State power to intervene in the economy and to carry out the post-war project of economic growth diminishes, so the local consensus around State policies is

The World Economic Crisis

undermined and the State increasingly resorts to more coercive forms of intervention to secure compliance. At the global level, the dominant role of the United States is challenged by the economic power of Western Europe and Japan and the newly industrialising countries, as well as the growing reach and independence of transnational corporations. This has reduced the effectiveness of international economic institutions and narrowed the policy instruments available to the United States. This is one of the reasons why the United States, to maintain its hegemony, has played up 'threats to security' and increased emphasis on demonstrations of military power, as in the deployment of Euromissiles or the increasingly visible naval build-up in almost all the oceans around the globe.

At the national level, States resort to repressive measures in the face of their inability to find alternative solutions to pressing domestic social and economic problems. Such measures include both physical and economic forms of repression, police violence and tight monetary policies. They also include the adoption of repressive ideologies in the name of national security or national integrity, generating fear of an external enemy or creating a warlike atmosphere or fears of disintegration in order to induce 'sacrifice' or acceptance of suffering.

Conflicts and wars have, of course, characterised the processes of uneven development, immiserisation, cultural dislocation, and political turmoil that have marked the post-war period. Although we describe this period as a period of 'world peace', it was actually a period of local wars and war preparations. The local wars caused enormous human, social, economic and ecological losses and reduced the development potential of the countries concerned. War preparations imposed tremendous military burdens, reducing resources available for the development of science and technology in new and creative directions. Yet as the germs of economic crisis multiplied, so the causes of war intensified, the tendency for war preparations increased and the ability of States to find non-military or non-violent solutions to conflict diminished, creating a vicious circle of militarism, repression and deterioration of economic conditions.

This list of phenomena, factors and processes which contributed to the current global crisis or which represented early symptoms of the crisis, can, of course, be extended and elaborated further. But it is probably sufficient to outline the 'pre-history' of the crisis in order to show that the latter was not just an accident or chance circumstance.

The global crisis, as many scholars point out, is not wholly new and needs to be explained also by reference to conventional paradigms, theoretical conceptions, economic policies and 'recipes' as well. Hence, the above *anamnesis* would not be complete and realistic if it did not include at least a brief discussion on the inadequacies of conventional thinking which was already visible in the fifties and sixties. The classical-neoclassical views on the harmonious operation of the world economy with its assumed equality of partners, automatic mechanisms for equilibrium, market spontaneity, specialisation according to 'comparative advantages', and capital mobility leading to equalisation in factor supply, productivity and income levels, all these induced the rise of a new school stressing inequalities, dependencies and disequilibria. And the conventional concepts of unilinear development, with its universal stages of growth, 'modernisation' by imitation, imported cultures, life-styles, ideologies and 'development agents', have gradually lost adherents. While the eruption and continuation of the global crisis highlighted the failure of these theories more than anything else, it also led to questioning of some other conceptions and paradigms, and dispelled many illusions.

The Eruption of the Crisis

The actual circumstances in which the global crisis can be said to have erupted did not help to identify the true cause of the crisis, but rather suggested only a misdiagnosis. In 1973-74, when the crisis actually erupted, there had been plenty of advance warnings. There had been a marked decline in investment waves, accelerated inflation and the growth of surplus capacity in several Western economies. All this was already visible in the late 1960s. But in the mid-1970s the crisis falsely appeared as the exclusive consequence of the oil price explosion, an 'artificial disturbance', by the Organisation of Petroleum Exporting Countries (OPEC), of the 'normal' mechanism and equilibria of the developed market economies and the international monetary and financial system.

Since the first oil price explosion was followed, temporarily, by increases in the relative price of certain other raw materials as well, this fact threw up apocalyptic visions about the absolute depletion of the non-renewable natural resources. One good example of this was the first report of the Club of Rome. But it also created illusions of a more or less general and lasting improvement of the terms of trade for some of the primary producing countries. Many economists shared the assumption that the Third World as a whole would be able, directly or indirectly, to gain from the crisis of the West, and that most of the primary producing countries would be immune to the harmful effects of this crisis. That only left out the energy-poor and over-populated countries with heavy import needs of oil and food, and without sufficient export capacities but, again, it was assumed that South-South cooperation would overcome their problems.

The success of the OPEC price explosion appeared as a hope and a model, an example to be followed by other primary resources-producing countries. However, it turned out that most other primary products, particularly agricultural raw materials and non-basic food products, had a substantially different position in the world market. Their demand elasticities showed quite different and often opposite behaviour, namely a high elasticity in the case of price increase and a rigid, inelastic reaction to rising prices. It was also very difficult for the producers to achieve concerted action, partly because production of such primary commodities was rarely concentrated in just a few countries and partly because of political differences between the producers. Soon, even the success of OPEC appeared to be limited. A considerable part of oil revenues had been absorbed by and recycled to the developed market economies. This was not only through bank deposits and direct or portfolio investments there, but also through imports of highly priced goods, particularly sophisticated armaments, technologies and luxury commodities. Moreover, the reaction of the major oil consumers to the oil price increases was to take strong energy-conservation measures. This, along with the effects of the recession, reduced the demand for crude oil. Besides, the continued structural weaknesses of the OPEC economies, as well as certain political conflicts and diverging economic interests within OPEC, also weakened its bargaining position. The fall in relative prices caused serious troubles and financial bottlenecks in oil exporting countries, which had launched large-scale investment programmes on the basis of high expectations about the future growth of oil revenues. The result is that at the time of writing there is a serious 'glut' in the oil market and oil prices are falling. Though a return to the era of depressed oil prices is very unlikely, the advantageous position of the oil exporters is only relative, and their opportunities for manoeuvre are rather limited. And this is likely to continue as long as their economic structure remains more or less one-sided.

Thus, only within a few years of the 'oil shock', it came to be realised that the crisis in the developed market economies could by no means be attributed merely to the change in the oil prices. And it also became clear that neither the majority of the developing countries nor the socialist countries could avoid the harmful effects of the crisis.

A 'Permanent' Crisis?

In developed market economies, despite some slight and temporary recoveries, the crisis has proved to be a lasting phenomenon with all the 'traditional' characteristics such as mass unemployment, under-utilised capacities, weak investment propensities, and sharpened competition. But there are also certain new features such as 'stagflation'. The average rate of unemployment in the OECD countries reached five per cent in 1974-75 and, without dropping below this level in the following years, went up to 5.5 per cent in 1979, over 6 per cent in 1980, over 8 per cent in 1981-82 and nearly 9 per cent in 1983 and thereafter. The number of unemployed in the developed market economies now exceeds 30 million. In addition, there has been a low rate of growth of GNP throughout the seventies and early eighties and a slow-down in the rate of growth of productivity.

The economic policies in many of these countries evolved to meet the consequences of the crisis seem to result in vicious circles. These problems, like the ones experienced earlier by the developing countries, point to the inherent interrelatedness of the world economic context and to the inability of individual countries to escape from the web. Protectionist measures, restrictive credit and trade policies, reluctance to increase official development assistance, etc., have actually led to a further deterioration in world market conditions, thereby hindering the recovery of the economies concerned. Instead of adjusting Keynesian regulation policies to the new conditions, the neo-liberal monetarist 'counter-revolution' has forged ahead and influenced government policy in several countries. This has tended to deprive national governments of even the available instruments of economic regulation. Depressed wages and reduced welfare expenditures, do lower the cost of wages and taxation for the individual entrepreneur. But they also tend to deteriorate further the market conditions by reducing effective demand. Moreover, the policy of increasing arms expenditures which results in the growth of a non-market sector, namely the military establishment, obviously conflicts with neo-liberal deflationary policy. Only a few countries with social democratic governments and competitive exporters such as Japan have escaped such vicious circles and have continued to experience economic growth.

By 1984, the effects of neo-liberal policies could be seen in a wave of strikes throughout Western Europe: in the long drawn out struggle against pit closures by the British miners in the face of massive police mobilisation; the strike of the IG Metall, the largest German (and indeed European) union for a 35 hour week; the opposition from workers to the Italian government's programme of wage reduction which gave rise to the biggest demonstration in Europe in post-war history; the steel and auto industries workers' strikes in France and so forth. But the lasting effects of the global crisis have proved to be the most harmful in the case of a majority of the developing countries. Their world market position and also their internal economic conditions have worsened, with the consequence that all the symptoms of crisis that have been observable since the late fifties have been aggravated while international assistance has declined.

The annual rate of growth of all developing countries still averaged about 5-6 per cent in the 1960s and in the first half of the 1970s, but it had dropped to $1-2$ per cent in 1982. In Latin

America, for example, for the first time since World War II, the aggregate real income and investment declined and *per capita* income decreased by nearly 3 per cent. The gravest consequences appeared, of course, in the poorest countries, most of them in sub-Saharan Africa, where agricultural output decreased steadily and produced a string of serious droughts and famines, leading to mass starvation.

Except for the major oil-exporters and a few others, the terms of trade of the developing countries have deteriorated further since the mid-seventies. Even the OPEC members have suffered considerable losses in the real or relative values of their export revenues, owing to international inflation, the changes in the exchange rates, the rapid rise in the prices of their imports, not to mention the recent decreases in oil prices. The losses from deteriorated terms of trade for the developing countries, except the oil exporters, amounted to around 34 billion US dollars in 1981 and 1982. The number of unemployed in these countries is estimated to be more than 400 million. The total external debt of the developing countries reached $750 billion in 1984.

These crisis symptoms are visible in all Third World countries, whatever the model of accumulation, with the possible exception of the four Asian newly industrialising countries (NICs). Because of their indebtedness, the Third World countries have no choice but to apply to the IMF. But the Fund imposes politically risky austerity policies that have proved socially disruptive and have driven the masses to the limits of their despair. The situation is worsened by the rising interest rates. The foreign debt crisis wrecks further havoc on the crisis-ridden Third World economies and on the lives of the masses. As a result, open discontent and revolt is multiplying throughout the Third World, witness the mass demonstrations in Argentina, Egypt, Sierra Leone, Liberia, Indonesia and the Philippines; general strikes in Bolivia and Peru; *coups d'etat* in Nigeria and Ghana; violent riots in Morocco, Tunisia, Santo Domingo and Haiti; supermarket lootings in Brazil; hunger marches in Chile and many other examples of mass protests against IMF imposed policies which have so far left hundreds of dead, thousands of wounded and incarcerated, and has stepped up State repression.

The socialist part of the world has also experienced, though as a whole on a far smaller scale than in the West or the South, the consequences of the world economic crisis and has faced unexpected difficulties. Though the average rate of growth of the Eastern European countries remained higher than that of Western countries in the seventies, some of these countries, e.g. Poland, entered a very deep economic and socio-political crisis. Others, such as Hungary, managed to keep their economies in relative balance and were able to restore an equilibrium that had been disturbed by external effects, but only at the cost of a radical slow-down in growth, almost to the point of stagnation; the salaried suffered a freeze, even reduction in real wages. As a matter of fact, all of the socialist countries of East Europe have suffered a considerable decrease in growth rate accompanied by trade deficits, increased foreign indebtedness and various degrees of inflation.

The unprecedented indebtedness of the socialist countries is the culmination of various factors, including imbalances in the pattern of production and consumption. These were caused by the demand 'explosion' which resulted from the demonstration effect of the Western consumer society, increases in the demand for modern technologies needed for the changeover to an 'intensive' stage of development, the deterioration (in a few cases a dramatic one) in the terms of trade and export facilities alongside a worsening of the credit facilities and terms in the international money market, and in some cases also caused by the sudden withdrawal of foreign deposits from their banks.

The indebtedness of these countries, however, unlike that of many developing countries, does not entail the same kind of consequences. Since most of the loans are used to contribute to productive and export capacities, they improve product competitiveness and thus serve to increase debt servicing capacities. Besides, the accumulation of debt by East European countries has not been accompanied and aggravated by the accumulation of foreign assets. So there is no latent self-generating indebtedness in their economies. Recent *ad hoc* government measures in East European countries, which combine strict import controls and export promotion, show that their debt problem is manageable. Socialist countries have, in fact, achieved a significant improvement in their trade balances and a reduction in their outstanding debt levels. But they have paid a price. Partly due to this focus on the restoration of balance, the rate of economic growth has been slow. The annual rate of growth of the net material product of these countries, which averaged 9 per cent in the late 1950s and more than 6 per cent in the late 1960s and the early 1970s, dropped to 4 per cent in the second half of the 1970s and decreased further to about 2 per cent in the early 1980s. The share of domestic consumption in national income has also considerably decreased in order to service the debt.

Restoration of economic equilibrium, revitalisation of economic growth and a flexible readjustment to the changed world economic conditions obviously require structural modifications in the economy and also reforms, including decentralisation to increase market responsiveness and stimulate local initiatives. However, steps in this direction often conflict with restrictive trade and investment policies with indebtedness and other difficulties standing in the way of promoting both exports and imports. They also conflict with the necessity for increased State intervention which often takes the form of *ad hoc* measures to save the economy from deeper crisis or disequilibrium. Here again, as in the case of other economies, a vicious circle appears.

But it is not enough to put the blame on international factors. Local factors also play a role in the deterioration of economic conditions, in the disturbance of specific equilibria or in slowing down growth. The business cycle, with its regular recessions, is an inherent feature of the capitalist economies. But neither the return, despite anticylical policies, of a deep economic crisis in the West, nor the deadlock in the South, nor new tensions in the economic management system of the socialist countries can properly and fully be explained independently and separately from each other.

The Causes of the Crisis

A correct and careful 'diagnosis' of the crisis must necessarily reveal, on the basis of our *anamnesis,* both those concrete factors and actual conditions that led to the eruption of the crisis and those fundamental contradictions in which a crisis originates.

Our prehistory of the crisis suggests the main concrete factors responsible for the eruption of the crisis. Let us recapture these.

First, substantial changes have taken place in the international power situation which have necessarily undermined the foundations and conditions for the operation of the 'colonial' type of international division of labour. (Without such shifts in international power relations the application of the oil weapon could hardly have been successful, even for a short time.)

Second, a redeployment process has been started, mostly by the transnational corporations, which has also brought about changes in the former colonial division of labour. This redeployment process has been very uneven, accentuating the differentiation within the Third World. Moreover, it has been spontaneous and unregulated and, therefore, not accompanied by an adequate readjustment in the developing countries. The sectoral imbalances of the world economy, namely between the primary resource-producing underdeveloped periphery and the manufactures-exporting developed centres, have not been eliminated; but rather aggravated, as in the case of the majority of developing countries. Or, they have been complemented by new sectoral disproportions which have induced a sharpening competition between the products of older Western industries and those of the newly industrialised developing countries or of the industrialised socialist economies.

Third, State intervention to regulate developed market economies has become increasingly ineffective. This is because of the hiatus between the national framework of the anti-cyclical regulation policy and the trend towards internationalisation of production and capital and towards economic integration and multilateralisation of economic relations. Similar problems have arisen in other countries, especially the developing countries. In the socialist countries, internal shortcomings, weaknesses or anomalies of the planning machineries, the anarchic and unforeseen changes and fluctuations of the world market have also caused disturbances in the system of planning and in the regulation of the planned economy.

A fourth factor which has also contributed to the eruption of the world economic crisis was the rise and spread of a 'consumer society' in the West, and its demonstration effect on other parts of the world. This 'consumerism' has been based upon the expanded credit system of the capital-rich Western economies as well as the cheap energy and raw material imports from the developing countries. The demands of the 'consumer society' have, therefore, not only exerted an increasing pressure on the world's non-renewable natural resources, they have also meant a built-in imbalance. For the consumer society is very vulnerable to interruptions in the supply of basic materials or changes in the terms of trade, as well as to domestic credit conditions. In addition, the demonstration effect of the 'consumer society' has biased the consumption and import patterns of Third World societies where the elites imitate Western consumerism. This has contributed to the aggravation of economic imbalances.

Finally, the crisis of the world economy is linked in many ways with global militarisation and its effects. Military spending has an important inflationary effect. The prices of weapons systems rise considerably faster than the prices of civilian goods and this pushes up the overall price index. Because military contracts in the West are generally cost-plus fixed contracts, profit rates are maintained even when there is a squeeze on profits elsewhere in the economy. In other parts of the world too, the military sector exerts an upward pressure on wages, because the higher relative salaries and wages there stimulate wage-bargaining in other sectors. Also, deficit-financing of military expenditures causes disequilibrium in the money supply. Besides the inflationary 'cost-push' and money-creation effects of militarisation, a 'demand-pull' effect can also arise, including in the economies with insufficient effective demand and 'over-production'. This is because the specific input-requirements or consumer needs of the military sector may be, at least temporarily, in inelastic supply or because production bottlenecks occur in certain spheres of manufacturing, especially in electronics, thereby causing price rises.

It is sometimes argued that military spending is an effective anti-cyclical Keynesian regulator. We see less and less evidence of this, since in both advanced industrial countries and the developing countries, military spending introduces structural distortion and long term economic disequilibrium. In developed countries, this is because of its uneven impact on different sectors of industrial growth. In

The World Economic Crisis

the developing countries military spending also reinforces external dependence of the economy which is accompanied by a regular income drain, balance-of-payment problems and cumulative indebtedness. Insofar as the growth of the military sector is accompanied by increasing imports of arms and other military-related commodities, by technologically dependent local arms production or by the stationing of locally financed foreign military experts (or a combination of these), it objectively contributes to the perpetuation of economic dependence with all its harmful consequences for equilibrium. Further, the redistribution of profit and income in favour of the military-oriented entrepreneurs, the income gap between military and civil salary earners and the relatively higher income level of professionals (both civilian and military) employed by the military sector have all contributed to the growth of already existing disparities and further growth of elite luxury consumption.

In the socialist countries, too, the arms race and militarisation influence development priorities, research activities and industrialisation policies (the growth and share of the heavy industry) and reduce the resources available for consumer production and investment, thereby affecting directly or indirectly overall development. The growth inhibiting effect of the military burden is particularly intensive in their case because of the nature of their economic system. Unlike capitalistic systems which tend to produce surplus capital and periodic unemployment, investment and employment opportunities in socialist countries tend to exceed the available capital and labour resources. Therefore, military investments, production and employment always compete with civilian ones and imply a net reduction from the resources available for economic activity that contributes to consumption and welfare of the people.

Over and above these concrete factors, there are basic or fundamental contradictions of the present world economic system which underlie the crisis. Three sets of such contradictions are distinguished.

The first set consists of those very general and fundamental contradictions which have always accompanied the development of capitalist national economies. Now *mutatis mutandis,* they also appear, and more obviously than ever, on a world scale.

Take for example, the contradiction between production and consumption. In the modern world, production is motivated by the search for profits, economic gains and advantages, while consumption is, on the one hand, limited by the unequal distribution of incomes and benefits in the international economy and, on the other, by the dominant centres of business-motivated production and elite-consumption. This contradiction, together with the continued existence of profound inequalities in world social relations, is manifested in the strange paradox of 'over consumption' in certain segments of the world society without a corresponding investment in the quality of life, and 'under-consumption' in other segments, both in the absolute sense (consumption is below subsistence minimum) and in the relative sense (effective demand is inadequate to ensure the full use of production capacities).

This contradiction is also reflected in the general distortion of the consumption pattern, with over-valued material goods. The heavy emphasis on material goods and the bias against cultural, intellectual, spiritual and artistic values are so evident on the international scene that the whole concept of an international division of labour, all the multilateral negotiations on international exchange and cooperation, and even the ideas of the restructuring of the world division of labour are practically reduced to known spheres of material goods production, or, at best, to those activities, such as research and technological development which are linked to production.

Another example of contradictions in this set is that between the increasingly collective 'world social' or transnational character of production and the 'individual' or national (State and/or private) appropriation of the economic surplus. Those who decide how the surplus is to be invested or consumed are not the same as those who produce the surplus nor are they necessarily sensitive to social needs. This is mitigated in societies where the major share of the surplus belongs to the community; nevertheless, even in those societies, the contradiction persists so long as producers and consumers do not have direct access to those State agencies which control the surplus. This gives rise to exploitation and unfulfilled needs.

The second set includes those contradictions which have emerged primarily on the world level. These include the dialectical contradiction between development and underdevelopment in the context of a worldwide division of labour between a dominant, developed centre and its dependent underdeveloped periphery. Despite economic growth at the periphery, the development gap and dependence relationship has persisted. This contradiction manifests itself and results not only in the structural distortions of the economy and society in the periphery but also in the bias of the economic structure and social behaviour at the centre. Certain irrational shifts in the pattern of economic activities, investments and expenditures, consumer preferences and choices of technology, as well as shifts in social stratification in the centre result from the centre's dependence on the resources of the periphery. These shifts sometimes go under the name of 'over-development'. The uneven development of the centre and the periphery of the world economy tends to exclude or undermine the equilibrium of the global reproduction process. This is because a proportional growth of the centre and the peripheries is indispensable if they are to serve as mutual markets.

Another contradiction of the capitalist world economic system which has characterised its long development and has sharpened in the most recent period is, again, the dialectical contradiction between national and international integration. Capitalism gave birth to integrated national economies, which provided a material basis for national identity and State power in core areas. Indeed, the development of the modern State was required to guarantee the integration of national markets, to maintain social stability and to ensure the free flow of resources within national boundaries. However, a fundamental contradiction developed between the global reach of capitalism and the geographical limitations of the nation-State. The tendency for international expansion and for the establishment of a world division of labour has always come into conflict with the geographical division of the world into nation-States. Britain, and later the United States, acted as a global State. But this role was periodically challenged both by other 'core' States and by the attempts of the nation-States in the periphery to create their own national economies. This explains the strange coincidence of, and also the conflict between, the advancing process of internationalisation and the modern struggle for national emancipation, national identity and national sovereignty. It also explains, among other things, the 'historical paradox' that socialism, intended originally to be an international, world-wide system, had to start its development within the national framework. Socialism has been surrounded by a more or less hostile international environment and therefore burdened by specific difficulties, deviations, and contradictions. There is also a potential conflict between socialist and national interests within socialist countries.

The third set of contradictions follow from the very beginning of the transformation of the system on the global level. They follow from the rise of anti-capitalist, socialist regimes in certain parts of the world. The national endeavours of an increasing number of developing countries to escape from their peripheral position in the world economy contribute to them. And they stem also from the growth of radical movements in advanced capitalist countries, as well as in other countries.

The contradiction between capitalist and socialist regimes affects in various ways both the domestic socio-political relations and the centre-pheriphery relations of the world economy. However, the historical antagonism between capitalism and socialism falsely appears as an inter-State, East-West, conflict which tends to obscure domestic social conflicts and conflicts among capitalist or socialist countries, West-West or East-East.

The contradiction between the nationalist movements of the developing countries and the centre powers of the world capitalist economy tends to modify the centre-periphery relations. This contradiction is often perceived as a 'North-South' conflict, a conflict between rich and poor nations. This is a misconception which blurs the real class conflicts and intra-national social gaps. At other times, the nationalist response is taken as a consequence of the 'East-West' conflict which in turn is solely attributed to an 'internal communist conspiracy'.

These contradictions, their interactions and persisting perceptions about them exert a destabilising effect on the world economy. They generate forces which can change the terms and conditions of international economic relations and which inject specific political dimensions, often with military implications, into the world economic situation.

Countervailing Pressures

What perspective and positive alternatives are open for the world economy as a whole or for individual countries and groups of countries to find a way out of the current deep rooted crisis? Can we envisage a recovery of the developed market economies and can such a recovery result in a new boom period in international trade which, if combined with a return to the policy of aid and trade of the First Development Decade, may promise a solution also to the grave problems of the developing countries? Does the example of the socialist countries, isolated for long from the world economy, show a positive alternative which can be followed by the developing countries? Could the delinking of developing countries from the industrialised world combined with a kind of collective self-reliance provide an appropriate answer, at least for the most seriously affected countries, to their immediate problems arising from the crisis? Is the idea of a new international economic order, if it is really put into practice by common efforts and political will, such that it will lead to a crisis-free, more egalitarian and democratic world? In what follows we shall deal with each of these issues.

A full recovery of the developed market economies would require the opening up of new sources of capital accumulation. Some economists consider that these could be found by making use of new technological developments in the field of micro-circuitry and in applying new discoveries in the chemical and biological sciences to meet new demands for resource conservation, environmental protection, food production and disease control among others. But this in turn would require major social and political changes, including both among the centre countries and between the centre and the periphery countries.

It is possible that a temporary recovery resulting from less far-reaching structural changes of the developed market economies could ease the most acute troubles of international trade and finance. Such a recovery, however, could easily lead to a further deterioration in the world market position of developing countries. After all, their market share and terms of trade worsened during the boom period of the 1950s and 1960s. Present shifts in the economic structure of the developed countries towards the tertiary sector, i.e., services, combined with technological and factor endowments as well as tariff policies, suggest that it is rather doubtful if the recovery of the advanced industrial countries would lead to increased imports from peripheral countries so as to stimulate their economic development. By the same token, without some real efforts to overcome underdevelopment, a lasting recovery of the developed countries is also doubtful.

The experience of the socialist countries and the effects of the world economic crisis on their economy have demonstrated both the possibility of a self-centred, socialist development with structural transformation under the conditions of the prevailing world economic order and its limitations. The socialist countries can claim undeniable achivements. They have brought about structural transformation of their economy and society; they have succeeded in the fields of industrialisation and rural transformation, national planning, education, science and technology, local research and development facilities, the elimination of pauperism and mass unemployment, the reduction of the income gap and traditional class differences, and much else. And they have been relatively less affected by the world economic crisis. These are obvious proofs of the feasibility of a self-centred development and economic transformation within a national framework. But it is also undeniable that there are difficulties, contradictions, distortions or roundabouts in socialist development. These have led to the partial relinking of socialist countries with the capitalist world economy. The subsequent appearance, in their economies, of certain crisis phenomena, e.g., sectoral imbalances, supply problems, structural and technological bottlenecks, disturbances in the planning and regulating mechanisms, cannot fully and simply be attributed to internal errors and mistakes, although internal factors may have aggravated them.

The possibility of adopting self-reliant policies, or of 'delinking,' for the developing countries depends both on the different forms of external dependence and on the extent to which external dependence is 'internalised' in the structure of the domestic economy.

There are substantial differences between various forms of economic dependence of developing countries. The most direct form of dependence is foreign ownership and control over key sectors, the 'commanding heights', of the economy. The more indirect forms include trade dependence, financial and monetary dependence, and technological, 'technical' education, and R&D dependencies. These different forms have effects on production and consumption structures and hence different consequences for income loss and international exploitation. These forms may support each other cumulatively and culminate in an extremely intensive dependence of the country concerned *vis-a-vis* a particular world power if the directions of the various dependence relations happen largely to converge. If they do not, different forms of dependence and different sources of dependency may offset the intensity of one another and may be used for lessening dependency.

The very complex and changeable patterns of dependence offer, therefore, considerable room to manoeuvre and provide opportunities for the dependent countries, by means of diversifying their partners or shifting from one form of dependence to another, to gain more independence even under conditions of dependence. The 'internalised' character of external dependence is manifested in the distorted and disintegrated socio-economic structure of the countries of the periphery. External dependence tends to reproduce itself in the relationship between a dominant, extroverted, and mostly foreign controlled enclave, and the partly destroyed, partly transformed and preserved, traditional sector within the same country. It follows from the dialectical relationship between the 'external' and 'internal' aspects of 'underdevelopment' that, even if all contacts with the outside developed world are cut off, the economy of the 'underdeveloped' periphery remains *de facto* extroverted and dependent, because of its distorted internal structure. As long as this internal structure prevails, it serves as a basis or actually paves the way for new forms of external dependence. Moreover, if the economy is unexpectedly cut off from the dominant partner, this may cause such serious disturbances in the economy that a crisis situation may develop which, as a result of increasing socio-political tensions, often manipulated from outside, leads to a *coup d'etat* or a collapse of the political regime. Such being the case, a successful reduction in economic dependence and a successful restructuring of the economy must go hand in hand.

Because of the dialectical relationship between economic dependence and structural deformations and because of the complexity of socio-economic relations of the underdeveloped periphery, many debates about 'alternative' choices of development policy which are abstracted from their multi-dimensional and dialectical context, prove to be meaningless. Debates about export-orientation or import-substitution, about types of comparative advantage, about whether to adopt capital-intensive or labour-intensive types of technology, about whether or not to cooperate with transnational corporations, or about the priority of industrial *versus* rural development are irrelevant unless they are situated in a broader discussion about fundamental social and political structures.

The idea of establishing a 'New International Economic Order' was a genuine demand by the developing countries for an overall reform of the prevailing international trade and monetary system. It was also a historic yardstick in international politics and a warning sign. But though the idea of establishing a 'new order' has matured further, hardly any progress has been made towards its implementation, except insofar as it has been used by transnational corporations and local elites as a rationale for industrial redeployment. The reason partly is the lack of political will but partly also the conceptual contradictions and inconsistencies which can be discerned in the relevant UN documents as well as in the approach towards negotiations.

There is a certain gap between the long-term objectives and the recommended concrete, short-term practical steps. The palliative measures of aid and preference take the pride of place in the negotiations while concrete actions for achieving structural transformation are largely neglected. The most serious short-coming is the very fragmentation, almost a kind of 'departmentalisation', of the interrelated issues, corresponding to the field of competence of the individual UN bodies, and leading to a chronic state of isolation within which the problems of North-South and East-West relations, NIEO and disarmament, are treated. Not only is there no holistic or global approach to the joint consideration of these problems but their appropriate negotiation is further hampered by the competition between negotiating fora.

Despite all this, there is no better alternative to the implementation of a programme for establishing a really new international economic—but only economic—order. There is the need for a radical shift in emphasis both in the programme and in the negotiations towards key strategic issues for achieving a truly holistic and global approach to these issues. Such a programme requires fundamental changes in the institutional structure and objective conditions. Institutional changes might include the 'democratisation' of the UN system and other international organisations, not only to ensure the participation of the government representatives of all nations but also to ensure the representation and participation of all genuine political forces and grassroot social movements of the world.

The objective conditions for equal and sovereign cooperation and democratic participation are related to progress in social and international emancipation. Since intra-national social inequalities and international inequalities are interrelated, a new international order cannot be achieved without internal changes also in the economies and societies.

Much more attention needs to be paid, both in the international cooperation policy, in the programmes of NIEO and global negotiations, and in the policies of all countries, to such strategic issues of global interest and their interlinkages as:

—the reorientation of production and consumption patterns towards real human needs and a radical reduction of socially unfavourable unproductive expenditures, such as armaments and luxury and conspicuous consumption;

—the redistribution of incomes in favour of the poor people both internationally and within nations;

—popular involvement and democratic participation of the masses in political as well as economic decision-making;

—the introduction of an effective international, multi-lateral and democratic control over the transnational activities, in keeping with both sovereign rights and duties of the States and with the democratic aspirations of the most affected strata within these States;

—the reduction and, as soon as possible, elimination of the great international assymetries in the pattern of distribution of foreign capital ownership and control over dynamic sectors of the economy;

—restructuring of the international division of labour in order to achieve a more symmetrical pattern of reproduction, thereby eliminating the technological oligopoly of developed countries and incorporating all the socially valuable non-material (cultural, artistic, educational) activities in organic parts;

—the promotion of regional integration as well as cooperation between regional organisations, in keeping with and in fact enhancing the integrity of each national unit and the creation or maintenance of internal organic economic and social processes;

—the gradual introduction of more elements of global planning and regulation of those activities and economic processes which affect the world as a whole or a majority of countries, and particularly future generations, through the democratisation of the UN system and of international organisations, while ensuring the maximum opportunities for local initiatives, self-determination and diversity; and lastly,

—the achievement through mutual efforts of global demilitarisation and establishment of a world security system.

These proposals amount to the proposition that transformation of the international State system is a precondition not merely for economic recovery but for 'development' in the fullest sense. Such transformation would include *simultaneously* a shift in power from the advanced industrial countries towards periphery nation-States (and global and regional institutions to achieve the same end) as well as a shift in power relations internally that would ensure increased accountability of all States to ordinary people. Such a new relationship between the State and civil society achieved both globally and nationally, could give rise to entirely new mechanisms for reconciling resources with need and for determining patterns of production and consumption. Producers and consumers must be directly involved in the process of transformation. *States cannot transform themselves.* The struggle for a New International Economic Order will, thus, have to be waged by labour movements, peace movements, civil rights movements, environmental and women's groups and movements for local autonomies and self-determination, and thus through the cooperation between all those political and social forces currently engaged in isolated struggles against different aspects of the current world economic crisis.

4

Conflicts Over Natural Resources

The world situation with respect to resource use is beset by confusion, short-run horizons of policy, special interests, and the distortions of the social and political order at both the local (State and regional) and global levels. Such circumstances create pressures that complicate the perceptions of reality and in the end turn anti-people. Broadly stated, the media, governments, and high finance have strong incentives to prevent a critique of existing patterns of resource use and a consideration of alternatives.

Besides, the vagaries of the market create confusion around the basic issue of scarcity. Those who prophesied the 1980s as a decade of tightening oil squeeze now seem silly in the light of the oil glut and falling energy prices. Indeed, across the whole range of commodities, including basic food and other basic needs, the present world situation seems more burdened by problems of surplus production than shortages. Of course, more sensitively interpreted, this situation is one of *apparent* over-supply and of a market mechanism that is unresponsive to those whose needs are not backed by purchasing power. As careful and objective surveys of global resources have consistently demonstrated, we are continuing to exploit the resource base of the planet in a manner that will confront future generations with severe, possibly unsolvable, problems. Even now it poses grave risks of environmental deterioration by way of desertification, flooding, ozone depletion, pollution, and accident-prone ultra-hazardous technological fixes (including nuclear power).

For instance, despite the apparent energy abundance of this decade, a growing dependence on nuclear power exists for an increasing number of critical States. This technology, especially in the light of the Chernobyl accident and other disclosures about hazards, is probably unfit for human society since it depends on too high a level of human competence sustained over time. Yet, it is regarded as 'impossible' to renounce nuclear power as an option for public policy. And if renounced, then, even in the immediate setting, a shortage of oil would re-emerge and in the meanwhile fresh recourse to timber, coal and water resources will be employed resulting in further erosion of forests, soils and river beds. That is, exceedingly dangerous adjustments underlie current patterns of resource distribution.

There exists also a tremendous cultural confusion that needs to be grasped. Both capitalism and State socialism rest upon romantic notions of human ingenuity that place no limits on the productive capabilities of the planet. Capitalists entrust the future satisfaction of needs to a market process, whereas State socialism relies upon a liberating class exerting overall control for the sake of society as a whole. Neither sees nature as a limiting obstacle to indefinite expansion. Both rest their hopes for the future on the ability of human ingenuity to exact more and more. It is a totally different view of resource policy than that of most indigenous peoples who were preoccupied with sustaining existing levels of resource flows in the face of an array of uncertainties associated with nature. No doubt, historically speaking, the gains registered by human ingenuity are impressive, and could be still more so, provided they are guided by an adequate ethos of fairness between social and personal demands and between present and future generations. In the end, resource use expresses and embodies prevailing political arrangements, and the former cannot be changed without changing the latter.

The recent period in human history contrasts with all the earlier ones in its strikingly high rate of resource utilisation. Ever expanding and intensifying industrial and agricultural production has generated increasing demands on the world's total stock and flow of natural resources. These demands are mostly generated from the industrially advanced countries in the North and the industrial enclaves in the underdeveloped countries of the South. Paradoxically, the increasing dependence of the industrialised societies on the resources of nature, through the quick spread of energy and resource-intensive technologies, has been accompanied by the spread of the myth that the triumph of modern technology heralds a decreased dependence on nature and natural resources. This myth is reinforced by an ingenious mode of disinformation: the introduction of long and indirect chains of resource utilisation leaves invisible the real material resource-demands of the industrial processes. Through this combination of myth and induced ignorance, the conflicts over natural resources are generally shrouded and ignored. The conflicts become visible only when the indirect resource demands of the upper classes dramatise the direct dependence of the poor on nature, which leads to the charge that it is the poor who are the prime cause of ecological degradation. But this contrast between the resource demands of the rich and the poor becomes more truly visible when resource-intensive industrial technologies employed by the rich are challenged by the communities occupying rural and tribal hinterlands whose very survival and well-being depends on the conservation of resources that are threatened by over-exploitation, or by ultra-hazardous operations.

Ecology movements emanating from the conflicts over natural resources and asserting people's right to survival are spreading in regions where the bulk of the natural resources are essential to provide basic needs for survival to the large majority of the population. The introduction of resource and energy-intensive technologies for the benefit of a minority undermine the material basis for their survival. The ecology movements thus underscore the more basic conflict between a just and sustainable pattern of resource use and an inequitable and hence unsustainable pattern of resource use.

We take natural resources as a broad ecological category subsuming all resources provided by nature. We also view conflicts in the broader sense of demands leading to societal tensions both at the tacit and at the explicit levels, including the special stances of violent and militarised conflicts over natural resources. Thus, we recognise the existence of conflicts even when they do not get transformed into violent confrontations.

Since natural resources are ecologically related and perform ecological functions in maintaining life support systems, conflicts over natural resources include resource utilisation based on conflicting resource functions. Such conflicts are often expressed as the clash between 'conservation' and 'exploitation' i.e., between ecological development and economic efficiency, between sustainable and non-sustainable utilisation. While conflicts over natural resources exist in both the North and the South, they are currently more complex and more pervasive in the South. The South is biologically richer in relation to both natural and human resources and, with its colonial legacy, has been cast in the role of supplier of renewable as well as non-renewable resources to the North. Given the increasing global demands on the vital resources of the tropical countries of the South, these regions have been the scene of various local, national and international conflicts centering around the question of utilisation, control and disposition of natural resources. As control over natural resources becomes a paramount issue in the drive for national and human survival, disagreements and differences of opinions, approaches and priorities as well as philosophies are brought out in the open. Conflicts over natural resources are, in essence, conflicts over the priorities and characteristics of development. They make explicit the diverse strategies and ideologies for development at the scientific, economic, political and cultural levels. It is these linkages between conflicts over natural resources with other concerns of 'peace and global transformation' that is the concern of this chapter.

Transition from Commons to Commodities

For centuries, vital natural resources like land, water and forest had been controlled and used collectively by village communities, thus ensuring sustainable use of these renewable resources. The first radical change in resource control and introduction of major conflicts over natural resources was associated with colonial domination of large parts of the world. The colonial domination systematically transformed common vital resources into commodities for generating profits and growth of revenues. The first industrial revolution was supported by this transformation of the commons into commodities that made resources in the South available for the industries of the North.

With the collapse of the international colonial structure and the establishment of sovereign countries in the South, it was expected that international conflicts over natural resources would decline and that policies guided by comprehensive national interests would emerge. However, resource-use policies have continued along the colonial pattern and have in fact got worse in the recent past, both with the elites in the Third World and their global trend-setters producing a major drain of natural resources, leading to another acute conflict among diverse interests. The most seriously threatened interest, in this conflict, appears to be that of the politically weak and socially disorganised groups of poor whose resource requirements are the lowest and whose lives are mainly supported directly by the products of nature outside the market system. Current changes in resource utilisation have almost wholly bypassed the survival needs of these groups. The changes are primarily guided by the cash and trade goals of the countries of the North and of the elites of the South. A major factor leading to drastic changes in resource utilisation is the increasing concern in the countries of the North for conserving their own natural resources through a global relocation of resource-intensive and pollution-intensive industries like chemicals, pulp and paper, steel and aluminium. In effect, environmentally damaging activities are located in Third World countries where regulatory standards are lower and the consequences of environmental decay are less likely to produce a political backlash. The desirability of such an industrial relocation from the point of view of the North has been openly acknowledged on several platforms dealing with economic policies.

The new global factors in resource transformation in the South create conflicts in two ways. First, they generate new pressures on the direct export of natural resources as primary goods to pay for the rising bills for civilian and defence technology imports. Second, the selective relocation of polluting and resource-intensive industries infringes upon the availability of these resources for the satisfaction of the needs of the local peoples. This deprivation results from the

Conflicts Over Natural Resources

outright appropriation of the resources, especially for the production of export-oriented goods and by polluting the resources. An analysis of the new directions of industrial growth in India, for example, indicates that these transformations and the resultant conflicts have already imposed severe costs on the people. During a period when India had been depending on food imports, the export of processed food rose by 28 per cent. The demand put on resources for processing is, thus, added to the demand put on resources like land and water for their production, and this further accentuates the conflicts over natural resources. Again, more recently, when the forest resources of India are on the verge of vanishing, forest-based industries like paper are slated for rapid large-scale expansion in their installed capacity as well as in liberalisation of export. An analogous situation exists in almost every Third World country.

Such shortsighted exploitation of natural resources conflicts with the importance of sound ecological policies. It is desperately important to sustain soil and water conservation as well as accord priority to local requirements for forest products like fodder, fuel, green manure, small timber, fruit and nuts, and emphasise basic human needs in working out resource priorities. Such priorities have to take account of the limits that constrain overall stocks of all resources, especially those that are sustainable.

The dwindling forest reserves have pushed the paper industries to look for newer bases of raw materials. As a result, in many parts of the world, a rapid transfer of food-growing land to the production of commercial woods like eucalyptus has taken place, a phenomenon termed 'social forestry'. This development has decreased the potential for food production in two ways. First, it has decreased the direct availability of existing cultivable land for much needed food production. Second, it has deepened the process of land degradation, particularly in the drylands, a process that reduces the long term potential for food production significantly.

Similarly, the expansion of energy and resource-intensive industries like aluminium or steel puts further demands on land and water. For the mining activities that support these industries, additional forest and farming land is being acquired and diverted from food production. The larger hydro-electric projects that are set up to generate power mainly for the growing industrial demands, in a similar manner, destroy the potential for the production of food by submerging vast areas of fertile land in river valleys.

Most of the protests against such transfer of basic resources have been local and disorganised so far. As a result, they have not exerted any serious influence on the formulation of national policies dealing with natural resources. With the advance of industrial growth in the years to come, these protests are almost certainly going to become more intense, reflecting the intensity of the conflicts over natural resources. These conflicts may not always take the form of peoples' ecology movements that hold the possibility of resolving these conflicts in a just manner. They may get distorted and express themselves as social conflicts along religious or ethnic lines, pitting militant groups against one another. Such a prospect means that resource scarcity and conflict are not treated as causes. Further, prospects for humane solutions are diminished to the extent that governmental actors and opinion-forming forces do not comprehend the possibility that a more constructive resource policy could restore social peace *and* meet the survival and development needs of currently antagonistic groups. That is, religious and ethnic conflict may, to varying degrees, be about resource allocations and scarcities. It is of great importance that social movements clarify the relevance of resource policy to the satisfaction of their goals and programmes.

Despite the similarity of the material processes of resource degradation, there is an important difference between the way in which conflicts over natural resources were handled in the colonial period and at present. Colonialism was characterised by transfers of, and increased access to, natural resources being made possible by direct political and military interventions, whereas the post-colonial period is characterised by a subtle use of a network of incentives and subsidies, and an ideology of development that is shared by the industrially advanced countries in the North and elites in the urban-industrial enclaves in the South. In the new political context of the post-colonial period the justifications of the resource utilisation patterns are hardly different from those in the colonial times. The suppression of challenges to these regressive approaches to the uses of resources is, in the first instance, linked to the ideology of 'modernisation' and its closely linked reliance on market mechanisms and capitalist calculations. This path is legitimised by a variety of means, including the claim of the rationality of science, the superior productivity of modern technologies and, above all, the rationality of modern economics on which 'modernising' modes of resource utilisation are based. Conflicts over natural resources must, therefore, be especially analysed in the light of the rationality and efficiency criteria employed to justify the present destructive patterns of resource utilisation in the name of 'development'. This analysis should examine specific impacts on poor people and on the overall health and prospects of the nation over an extended period.

We have already observed that conflicts over natural resources began to be generated by transformation of free, common resources accessible to the whole society into 'inputs' (raw materials for production) over which a minority established exclusive control and to which the general population lost access except through the market. Such transformation of the 'commons' into 'commodities' has become a global trend which is, in our times, generating a wide array of conflicts over natural resources and threatening peace at the very grassroots of societies.

Model of Contemporary Science and Technology

We believe that science provides one approach to knowledge of reality and that technology provides the means to transform natural resources into forms useful to human society. But the specific manner in which the dominant forms of contemporary science and technology have evolved poses serious and subtle problems in relation to resource policy. The tightly integrated link between science and technology is highly problematic. It is not mainly the quest for truth but the search for technological 'achievements' that today legitimises science. And the relative values of these achievements tend to reflect militarist priorities and other distortions arising out of the socio-economic structure of modern States. Pursuit of scientific knowledge today is no longer an open-ended search for nature's mysteries; the origins of research funding frequently taint the whole undertaking of scientific inquiry. Governments and multinational firms invest heavily in goal-directed research with specific technological ends in mind. The modern science-and-technology model is thus not characterised by 'free' discovery followed by subsequent incidental uses and 'applications'. The 'use', in fact, is predefined and is the goal which generates knowledge.

Such integration of science and technology demands that we take the science and technology system as a conceptual category rather than conceive of science and technology independently. As integrated by modern structures of power and wealth, science and technology provide the principal tools to determine and justify how resources are to be utilised, and misutilised. When new systems of science and technology impact upon an area of natural resource use, conflicts emerge at various levels. Most of these technological shifts are the consequence of the central drive to achieve 'modernisation'. Thus, the modernisation drive in agriculture, one expression of which has been the 'green revolution', introduced new methods of production, new philosophies of growth and new ways to generate and manage production. All of these outcomes cause conflict. The competition for scarce land, the distribution of its products, and the allocation of any surplus lay bare the roots of conflict that are present in the agricultural sector. Many of the most intense conflicts over land in recent years can be traced back to the almost forced transformation of subsistence farming in favour of commercialised and modernised production in large parts of Asia, Africa and Latin America.

The dialectical contradiction between the role of natural resources in production processes to generate growth and profits, and their role in natural processes to generate stability and satisfy needs is evident if we consider some ecology movements. These movements have demonstrated that the perception, knowledge and value of natural resources reflect the outlook of different interest groups in society. The politics of ecology is, thus, intimately tied up with the politics of knowledge. For subsistence farmers and forest dwellers, a farmer or a forest possesses the basic economic function of soil and water conservation in relation to energy and food supplies. For the industrial promoters the same farm or forest has mainly the function of being a mine stocked with needed raw materials. These conflicting approaches to natural resource use, based on their diverse functions in distinct social systems, are dialectically related to conflicting perceptions and knowledge about natural resources. The knowledge of forestry developed by forest dwelling communities, therefore, evolves in response to the economic role assigned to the forest. In contrast, the knowledge of forests developed by forest bureaucracies to satisfy industrial requirements is predominantly guided by the dollar value of efficiently maximising raw material production.

The way nature is perceived is, therefore, related to the pattern of utilisation of resources. Modern scientific disciplines that provide the currently dominant forms of perception of nature have generally been viewed as 'objective', 'neutral' and 'universally valid'. These disciplines are, however, no more than particular responses to particular economic interests. This kind of economic determinism influences the content and structure of knowledge about natural resources, which, in turn, validates particular forms of resource utilisation at the expense of others. In essence, profit-maximising is validated and needs-satisfaction is treated as irrelevant.

Resource utilisation in the non-sustainable growth model of economic development is related to a particular way of looking at nature and natural resources. Two central assumptions underlie this reductionist perception of nature:

(i) that natural resources are isolated and non-interacting collections of individual resources; and
(ii) that natural resources acquire economic value only when commercially exploited, thereby becoming susceptible to market valuation.

We identify this approach to nature as reductionist for two reasons. Firstly, it reduces nature to its constituent parts, and takes no account of the relationship betweeen the parts and the structure and functions of the whole. Secondly, it reduces economic value to something produced only with technology and capital inputs for the market and takes no account of the conservation of resources, or their use to satisfy basic human needs. But our concern is to promote resource policies that take account of what ordinary people, especially those belonging to deprived groups, need and want.

Reductionism and specialisation are twin attributes of the dominant Western orientation toward science and technology. From the first reductionist assumption that resources are fragmented in nature arises the fragmentation of the natural sciences. The properties and functions of nature that receive predominant attention by specialised scientific disciplines are those that can be reduced to one-dimensional properties of individual resources. Properties of nature that arise through interrelationships of resources, have, until very recently, rarely been even perceived or investigated. The main scientific tests are measurements of properties of natural systems usually involved in a 're-realisation of ordinary reality', a rupture of relationships between resources, and a reconstruction on the basis of these truncated measurements. The blinkers of reductionism prevent access to knowledge and understanding of the properties and functions of natural resources generated by their interrelationship.

Reductionist profiles of reality thus falsify, by their very neglect, the holistic properties of natural systems even while laying claim to be the guardians of objectivity and scientific truth. When natural resources are perceived, and policies framed, in accordance with the claims of reductionist science, science itself becomes epistemologically unreliable for explaining the more complex behaviour of living systems. These systems possess a dominant tendency towards interaction, a reality associated with the ecological perspective. Reductionism in natural science has contributed to, and has, in turn, been influenced by, reductionism in economics. Functions and uses of natural resources that are not valued in the market are, as a consequence, denied value in economics and thus become invisible in natural science.

In spite of being created and sustained by a restricted set of transitory economic values, reductionist natural science posits itself as universally and objectively applicable to all economic uses and functions of natural resources. The universalisation of such restricted and partial knowledge has the further and adverse consequence of marginalising knowledge systems that have been generated over millenia within the context of multi-purpose and multi-functional resource utilisation. Such integrated but less articulated knowledge systems have been characteristic of most traditional societies that

Conflicts Over Natural Resources

have generally and successfully used their knowledge for utilisation of natural resources in ecologically stable and sustainable ways. The ecological awareness of these communities has, however, often been rejected as 'superstition', 'myth' and 'irrationality' because the framework of ecological explanation has always relied upon literary or religious metaphors. As a result, the embodied ecological wisdom of the people has been rejected or ignored; it seemed not to fit into the reductionist paradigm of rationality.

It is instructive to contrast the reductionist approach to a holistic one. The latter is familiar to many traditional cultures. In 1854, when the European colonisers wanted to buy land from the original inhabitants of America, Chief Seattle had this to say:

> It will not be easy. For this land is sacred to us. The rivers are our brothers, they quench our thirst. The air is precious to the red man, for all things share the same breath—the beast, the trees, the man, they all share the same breath. The white man does not seem to notice the air he breathes. Like the man dying for many days, he is numb to the stench. The earth does not belong to man, man belongs to the earth, this we know. All things are connected like the blood which unites our family. Man did not weave the web of life, he is merely a strand in it. What he does to the web, he does to himself.

The Conflict Between Profits and Survival

The stranglehold of commercial and marketplace notions over use-value of the most basic natural resources can be illustrated by the worldwide penetration of agribusiness. Agribusiness is playing a part in the global transformation of utilisation of croplands, and is generating conflicts over land-use and ownership—both tacit and explicit. During the Marcos era in the Philippines, for example, multinationals such as Del Monte, Dole and United Brands exerted almost unchallenged control of the Filipino banana and pineapple export industry. Del Monte farms in Kenya deliver to consumers in the North jet-shipped pineapples. In both cases, land which was growing staple crops for local consumption has been diverted to cash crops that leave the people more vulnerable than before. As the Sahelian drought was getting worse in the 1960's, Senegal was loading one DC-10 aircraft three times a week between December and May with green beans, melons, tomatoes, eggplant, strawberries and paprika, destined to satisfy gourmet tastes in Stockholm, Paris and Amsterdam. Villagers who occupied the land needed for these new vegetable farms were evicted in large numbers by the Senegalese Government. In spite of all that one hears about starvation among Senegalese and other West Africans, the great bulk of what agribusiness produces is still flown out of this distressed region for consumption by the European Common Market.

This is bad enough, but there is a more grotesque angle. In 1974, European governments spent $53 million to destroy European produced vegetables so as to keep up the prices. The market prices for green beans in Europe had fallen lower than the cost of picking, packing, and air-freighting the produce of agribusiness operations located in Senegal. We cannot get away from the irony: if Senegal, to give only one example from the Sahel, can grow vegetables for the European market, it can surely grow food for its own people. Starvation in Africa's semi-arid regions, it turns out, is at least as much a man-made and market-made phenomenon as it is a consequence of natural disaster.

Some of the agribusiness companies deliberately enter those countries which do not have a local market for the products they wish to produce so as to assure a continuous supply because of the absence of a competing local demand. They regard Africa generally as a future vegetable producer and exporter in the world—for Europe and possibly America. Studies by the World Bank confirm that countries like Senegal and Mauritania provide excellent future regions for mango, eggplant and avocado exports. Africa's attraction to agribusiness also stems from its proximity to highpaying importers in the Middle East. With their technological approach, agribusiness companies see much of Africa as containing vast acreages of unutilised and underutilised land. Ethiopia, in spite of recent drought and starvation, has for instance, great potential for land-use development. In some of these countries, large uncultivated royal and church-owned estates are seen as an open invitation to agribusiness that is always on the lookout for cheap productive land. Although for many of these countries roads and other infrastructure components are poorly developed, the World Bank and other foreign aid projects are obligingly 'opening up' the countryside. Even their governments that seek such projects generally do not realise, or do not want to realise, that the land could, in the alternative, be opened up to local inhabitants. In some cases agribusiness promoters do not undertake production for their own countries, but for third country markets. A case in point is the arrangement made between the Ethiopian and Italian governments in early 1970's by which the Italian firm MAESCO produced alfalfa in Ethiopia to feed livestock in Japan. MAESCO's plantations happen to be located in areas that were the best grazing lands in the country. Thousands of Ethiopians died of starvation in 1973 together with their herds of camels, cattle, sheep and goats. In the same year, MAESCO began raising on the same lands its own cattle and sheep for export.

Some of the most sophisticated planners in the world evidently believe that offering science and technology and know-how to a predominantly peasant population in the world is *the* answer to world hunger. However, in reality, an uncritical application of these policies based on scientific and technological know-how imported from abroad can actually generate hunger by diverting resources away from the poor to the rich. The science and technology of agribusiness helps in linking up 'underdeveloped' country farms with overseas food and other agricultural products, creating a Global Farm supplying a Global Supermarket. The process creates a competition between the world's hungry people and the well-fed and overfed. Firstly, the production from scientific farming is often not always calibrated with basic food needs. Secondly, producing staples does not assure their consumption by those that need them or by those living nearest to the locus of production. Produce is usually placed on an emerging global supermarket where the rich and the poor reach for it on the same shelf. However, without the necessary purchasing power, no one can carry food outside the store. Dogs and cats in the richer countries can and do easily outbid the world's poor and hungry. Market priorities and human priorities move at cross-purposes.

The emerging global supermarket threatens to establish a dangerous form of food 'interdependence' in a world of unequals, generating unintended conflicts. Globally oriented agribusiness is far less interested in the staples specifically consumed by the poor—like maize (corn), beans, rice, wheat, sorghum, yams or millets, than in luxury crops, like asparagus, cucumbers, strawberries, tomatoes, mangoes, chicken, squash and flowers. The unequal and conflicting demand for land between the staples and exotic products causes ecological disturbances to the extent that global cash crop production exceeds the resource capability of local ecosystems. Under such pressure land use can become unsustainable, and the poor and the under-represented of the world are deprived of their basic food requirements both in the present as well as in the future. It is significant that the acuteness of these deprivations and conflicts can be often related to the introduction of new scientific techniques by agribusiness that are explained away as a short term price for increasing overall productivity.

The concept of 'productivity' of technologies is a very limited one, linked to a market-oriented calculus of measurement based on profits and losses and return on capital. Productivity is actually an ideological concept. When it is universalised, all other costs of the economic process become invisible. The invisible forces that contribute to this increased 'productivity' of a modern farmer or factory worker come from the increased, often excessive, or unwise, uses of natural resources.

Amory Lovins has described such productivity as the amount of 'slave' labour at work in the world in our times. According to his calculations, each person on earth on an average, possesses the equivalent of about 50 slaves, each working a 40 hour week. The global energy conversion from all sources (wood, fossil fuels, hydroelectric power, nuclear energy) at the present time for all human beings is approximately 8×10^{12} watts. This is more than 20 times the energy content of the food necessary to feed the present world population at the FAO standard diet of 3,600 calories per day. According to Lovins:

> In terms of workforce, therefore, the population of the earth is not four billion but about 200 billion, the important point being that about 93 percent of them do not eat conventional food. The inequalities in the distribution of this 'slave' labour

between different countries is enormous, the average inhabitant of the USA for example, having 250 times as many 'slaves' as the 'average Nigerian'. And this, substantially, is the reason for the difference in efficiency between the American and the Nigerian economies: it is not due to the differences in the average 'efficiency' of the people themselves. There seems to be no way of discovering the relative efficiencies of Americans and Nigerians: if Americans were short of 249 out of every 250 'slaves' they possess, who can say how 'efficient' they would prove themselves to be?

The resource and energy-intensity of modern production processes shows that the population factor is less significant than the intensity of resource utilisation in the production and consumption patterns of human societies. Thus, although the countries of the South have a much larger population than those of the North, the industrial quarter of the world uses more grain in total than the other three quarters put together. The net grain use per person in the industrialised countries is now three or four times higher than in the developing countries. This disproportion is not due mainly to the direct consumption of food. It is a consequence of heavier meat consumption in the richer countries. Livestock in industrialised countries consumes about 67 per cent of grain, while only 33 per cent is eaten directly by humans.

For the individual meat producer and the agribusiness system of accounts this is an 'efficient' method of operation. But for the social and material well-being of human society as a whole, this pattern of food production and consumption is grossly inefficient, as well as unsound ecologically, and short-sighted. For beef production, ten calories of energy are needed as input to give one calorie of food as output. It is only energy subsidy available to an industrialised economy that makes such a counterproductive and wasteful process appear efficient. Besides being wasteful of energy, the process also wastes other resources. It bypasses the natural advantage of cows in converting low protein food such as green fodder into high protein food. Feedlot production of beef also converts the economically valuable animal waste into a pollution hazard by isolating animal husbandry from farming.

The fragmentation of components of the farm ecosystem, and the integration of these separate components with distant markets and industries, is a characteristic of modern 'scientific' agriculture. The most common justification of the introduction of this system of food production is that it raises agricultural productivity. The high 'productivity' of modern agriculture, however, turns out to be a myth when total resource inputs are taken into account. The social and ecological costs with respect to the manufacture and use of fertilisers, pesticides and labour-replacing energy and equipment are rarely taken into account. The appearance of efficient, gainful agriculture is sustained by suppressing its wasteful and unsound features. If the energy used to provide all inputs in modern farming are deducted from the food calories produced, modern agricultural technologies are found to be shockingly inefficient. At the turn of the century, even in the countries of the North, one calorie of energy invested in land generally yielded more than one calorie in food value. Now several calories must be put into land to make it yield one. In real terms, agriculture has been deteriorating under the impact of modernising efficiencies.

The inefficiency in materials utilisation within production processes which rely on resource-intensive technologies can be illustrated by the production of soda ash, an important industrial material. In the 'Solvay' process for the production of soda ash, two raw materials are used, sodium chloride and limestone. All of the limestone used in the process is eventually eliminated as waste material. Twenty-five percent of the sodium chloride is also lost as unreacted salt. From the balance, the acidic half is further lost and only the basic (alkaline) half goes into the final product. Thus only 40 percent of the raw materials consumed are actually used. Furthermore, these waste products pollute land and water resources. The economy of the process is artificially made to appear efficient by granting concessions in the procurement of limestone, salt and fuel and by further public sector concessions with respect to land, transport, and infrastructure. It is such disguised subsidies that make a grossly inefficient process appear efficient. The trick is to bias the system of accounts in favour of modernising technologies.

Economic concessions related to natural resources utilisation and to certain types of economic activity on the part of privileged groups give those activities an unfair advantage over the activities of less privileged groups who compete for the same resources to satisfy far more basic needs. But when guided by the narrow and distorted concept of efficiency, technological change continues in a direction that is more resource-intensive while displacing labour. The upper limit of this economic logic is reached when human labour is rendered superfluous and dispensable in productive processes. If this logic persists, the survival of a vast majority of the people is threatened both by removing them from the process of production and by endangering the resource base that satisfies their basic material needs for survival.

We believe that a reconceptualisation of the concept of productivity is essential for the formation of socially responsible and ecologically sustainable policies towards the use of natural resources. Without this reorientation the well-being, and even the survival of the human society as a whole, will be in grave danger. Such a reconceptualisation must necessarily facilitate shifts in the criteria for technological choice, so that technologies for resource transformation that do not damage productive capacities of nature are preferred, as are those making the fullest use of human capabilities.

The lack of a theoretical recognition of the two ends of the economic process, its beginning in natural resources and its end in basic human needs, has shaped the current paradigm for economic and technological development that views current industrial production as an end in itself and demands more and more natural resources regardless of social and ecological consequences. One set of demands for resources originates in the minimum survival needs of the people. Another set of demands originates in the imperatives of economic growth that support affluent and wasteful lifestyles based on artificially generated non-vital needs of the privileged elite. One direct result of this contradiction is that rapid changes are taking place in the international distribution of resources and the relocation of productive capacity. The emerging patterns reinforce our view that resources needed for survival in the South are being increasingly appropriated to produce commodities to enrich further the standards of living in the North. We speak about general tendencies because the precise extent and implications of the transfer of resource-intensive and pollution-intensive industries from the North to the South has yet to be adequately studied and documented. Nor is there enough analysis available on the destruction of minimal life support systems of local populations as a consequence of the complex network of global relocations of industry. This process is also occurring between rich and poor regions within countries all over the world.

The economic and political power of the privileged elites assures their control over innovative technologies for the use of natural resources, a control exerted frequently at the further expense of the needs of the people. This new process of the transfer of control over natural resources within countries often takes place through State-sponsored programmes which go under the name of development of 'backward areas'. Increasingly, global resource systems are being managed by multinational corporations. More and more goods are now made in the poor countries of the South operating under guidelines and criteria set by headquarters in the North, and most of these goods are destined for the markets in the North that aspire to attain a 'post-industrial look', minimising the soot and grime of industrialisation. Unequal access to and control of the world's resources, reinforced by unequal access to and control of science and technology, thus aggravates conflicts over natural resources. Understanding this is vital for the entire process of global transformation.

Countervailing Tendencies
These threatening trends are, in some instances, being challenged by peoples' movements for control over natural resources, for basic needs, as well as by peoples' movements for approaches to science and technology informed by ecological, ethical, and social factors. The struggles of traditional fishermen in India and Malaysia against mechanisation of trawling, the struggles of tribal communities and forest peoples in large parts of Asia against the forest-technocracy, the struggles of peasants and farmers in almost all countries of the South against factory-farming are indicative of these countertrends.

In the countries of the North the countertrends manifest themselves most dramatically as the 'Green' or ecology movements, or the more eclectic alternatives movements. These movements are associated with the peace movement, objecting to the militarisation of research and development activities and resource allocations. If these countertrends grow stronger, the dialectic between prevailing modes of science and technology and alternative patterns of resource use could become very intense, and the outcome of ensuing struggles will determine whether a liberating peace is possible.

The Crisis of 'Development'

In the previous chapter, we have discussed at some length the global economic crisis, although with some acknowledgement of regional variations. The three major elements of the global economic crisis are debt, unemployment, and the destruction of nature's wealth. Unemployment and debt have affected countries of the North as well as the South. The United States, the world's 'strongest' economy is also the planet's biggest debtor with net foreign liabilities of about $120 billion at the end of 1985. However, for the debtor nations of the South, while foreign debt is only a loss, the ecological costs are disastrous. The roots of the global economic crisis are the same, but the symptoms, the prognosis and the prescriptions for a solution vary a great deal in different regions.

It is clear, then, that when it comes to natural resources, it is not possible to talk of *global* crisis. Resource crises of different regions and different social sectors within regions vary enormously from one another; to make global generalisations is both unhelpful and misleading. For most of the countries in the industrialised affluent North, the contemporary economic crisis is mainly a crisis of the post-World War II technological paradigm which the governments and corporate elites seek to overcome through rapid relocation of capital, development of electronics, automation, and international division of skilled labour. The economic crisis is principally translated by them into technological and financial parameters. The relocation of industry in more acceptable settings is part of this process of creating a new technological paradigm in the North, as well as lessening the environmental and social burdens arising from careless patterns of industrial development. That crisis affects the North as well as the South.

However, the South also suffers from its own economic crisis, which has global roots, but is more deeply felt in the Third World because it impinges on the very survival of the masses. The global money-lending system first sets the debt trap for the South through its 'development aid' packages and then leaves the Southern economies in ruin through the servicing of debt. Globalisation drives Third World countries to export more and more primary produce to reimburse bigger and bigger debts.

Thus, external debt for Latin America, Africa and Asia rose from $94.3 billion to $129.3, $230.7 to $355.6, and $84.7 to $274.8 respectively between 1980 and 1984 and the burden of debt servicing alone had started crippling these economies. During the same period, servicing of debt rose from $75.9 billion to $100.5, $91.8 to $128.3, and $73.6 to $112.9 for these regions. The growing problem of debt generates conflicts over natural resources in the Third World at three levels. At the most obvious level, it generates 'price wars' among the countries in the context of crumbling primary commodity prices. These wars are not waged with the global money-lenders like the World Bank which also make commodity price forecasts and prescribe solutions to the debt problem through recipes of increased exports and over-production. Third World countries, all victims of these strategies, then run into conflict with each other to maintain a place in a shrinking global market. At another level, resources like land are diverted from basic needs satisfaction to cash-crop or commodity production at the international level, making basic resources like food less accessible to the poor within each country.

Finally, at a deeper level, commercialised land use and cash-crop production violate ecological laws of sustainable productivity. Both impacts turn into an economic crisis for the poor which is largely invisible on the global canvas. It arises partly from resource destruction, or diversion of natural resources away from the poor, with the consequent loss of means of livelihood and employment. Except for spectacular disasters the crisis stays largely invisible because it affects only the informal and unorganised strata of society and because it hits hardest the marginal communities whose only resource has been their capacity to live from the natural environment. These strata and communities exist only at the remote periphery of world consciousness, the strong philanthropic response to hunger in Ethiopia (or Bangladesh earlier) notwithstanding.

We have already discussed the relocation of productive capacities and the creation of 'global factories and farms' with agriculture being transferred from peasants into the hands of agribusiness. Factory manufacture, similarly, frequently involves the transfer of production from the artisans and crafts-persons to large resource-intensive, energy-intensive and labour-displacing industry. Once more, this involves scarce resource being used to stimulate over-consumption of a few instead of being directed at the basic needs of the many. Such massive displacement of the crafts and the subsistence agriculture throughout the South severely threatens communities of artisans and the subsistence farmers. It menaces their survival and is directly linked to the ecology crisis through the policy-laden allocations of natural resources. It is also directly linked to the imposition of measures which are viewed as 'solutions' to the visible economic crisis of the privileged. Yet some of these measures are also offered as solutions of the overall circumstances of Third World countries, including mass misery. These solutions, labelled 'development projects', can be found in all areas of resource utilisation. Experience over the last four post-war decades has shown that such guided 'development' generates additional resources that benefit elites, while destroying the main resource basis of subsistence of the poor, which is nature. For the poor, development has come to mean an aggravating condition of economic, cultural and environmental instability.

Conflicts over natural resources and mechanisms for their resolution, when interpreted against the background of economic conflicts, can best be understood as confrontations between two fundamental types of economic organisation, one based on financial and technological inputs and the consequent wastage of resources, and the other based on ecologically sustainable austere and prudent appropriation of natural resources. The rich countries and the elites of the poor countries have become utterly dependent on short term economic growth. The poor of the poor countries have to pay for it through ecological degradation, which in effect erodes their capacity for survival based on knowledge of, and access to, local resources.

In the conventional model of economic development, poverty is explained as arising from the lack of sufficient production based on modern technologies. The higher efficiency and productivity generated by the modern scientific and technological production systems are expected to lead to higher rates of growth which, in turn, are supposed to enlarge the overall product enough to banish poverty over time. Poverty as the consequence of the lack of modern technologies is a formula which reflects the pervasive assumption in the most influential forms of development theory. The much used metaphor for development based on growth alone has been that of a pie; it needs to grow bigger so that each stratum of national and international society can have a larger slice of it. The socio-economic problems of poverty and inequality are treated as 'technical' impediments that can be resolved by technical solutions. Economic growth based on modern technologies is presumed to provide an automatic assurance that economic development is for the benefit of all.

After three decades of planned development in a large number of countries in the South that have meticulously adhered to the growth model of development, we now see obvious and deep cracks in the confidence and hope of peoples in the previously unquestioned supremacy of technological 'fixes'. Even in some rapidly industrialising States like Brazil that have recorded phenomenal growth-rates, the results have not always helped to alleviate the misery of the poor. The growth rates have turned out to be for short periods leaving behind debt burdens for much longer periods. In many circumstances, the quality of life for the poor has degenerated further, and a feeling of anti-Western alienation has taken hold. In particular, as previously discussed, the introduction of more 'efficient' technologies in areas like agriculture, forestry or fishing has put the biological survival of the poor at stake, especially in the countryside. To be sure, some Asian NICs have achieved growth that has benefited all sectors, particularly where the process of industrialisation has been preceded by land reform and where the governing process has been reasonably free from large-scale corruption. But such success stories remain only small islands stranded in an ocean of disappointment.

The increasingly visible shortcomings of modernisation have given rise to a second model of development which distinguishes between growth of the economic 'cake' and solution for the problem of poverty. It rejects the view that poverty is a technical problem; poverty, instead, is treated as a political problem of distribution which requires a restructuring of power relations in society to ensure a better allocation of the benefits of growth. The elites, this model explains, coerce the less powerful and the less privileged to accept much smaller slices of the cake. Accelerating poverty is due to the fact that the poor have been 'left out' of the process of development; as a result they have not been able to participate in sharing the material benefits of growth. The prescription for the removal of poverty in this model is to incorporate the less privileged in the growth process. Development strategy must include the redistribution of benefits.

This reformist outlook rarely exhibits concern for the redistribution and assessment of costs, especially the ecological costs imposed by resource-intensive technologies. The reformist model, for example, is insensitive to the ecological impact associated with polyfibre production, the destruction of soil productivity through eucalyptus farming for pulp-wood, or the destruction of water resources through pollution. The solution to the problems of underdevelopment proposed is a mechanical redistribution of that power which is embodied in the ownership of the means of industrial production, by simply shifting the same in favour of those who do the work. Such a populist approach to development would recommend that the production of eucalyptus trees should be combined with operations of polyfibre factories, and that the overall benefits be distributed for the sake of the poor. In another variant, ownership is devolved upon labouring sectors to benefit more directly from modernisation.

The rapid spread of the people's ecology movements for survival in large parts of the world, however, has much more to tell us. The movements affirm that the marginal and poor peoples have indeed suffered from the present patterns of development. But they reject the notion that the poor have been 'left out' of the process of development. They know that the poor and the marginal people have, in fact, been integral parts of that process since almost without exception these vulnerable sectors have borne the largest and most immediate costs of resource destruction and allocations. They have come to appreciate the growing escalation of the 'invisible' costs of resource destruction and allocations if expansion of production were to be based on resource and energy-intensive technologies. That is, if these costs were taken into account and subtracted, then many modern industrial enterprises would no longer be 'efficient' or 'profitable'. The ecology movements tell us further that the cake has actually shrunk in terms of resources vital for the survival of the peoples because of the growth of environmental decay and resource-degrading technologies. The problem of poverty and underdevelopment is understood by these movements as arising from, or sustained by, ecological destruction at the material level.

This interpretation by social movements has given rise to a third model for the political economy of development. This model recognises that resource-intensive growth accentuates poverty and inequality. It sees an ecological and material relationship between growth measured by financial yardsticks and the destruction of natural resources and nature's productivity at the human level of societal existence. While the cake apparently 'grows' when measured in terms of gross *national* product, it actually shrinks in terms of gross *natural* product. Politically, the contradiction between growth and resource destruction forms the material basis for the increasing prosperity of a minority and the increasing destitution and deprivation of the majority. The gains accrue to the economically and politically powerful, while the associated costs of ecological destruction, which remain largely undisclosed and unacknowledged in the form of negative externalities, are borne by the economically and politically most vulnerable nations, communities, races, gender and their children.

Resource-intensive growth, thus, generates increasing poverty and underdevelopment diverting or destroying resources needed for survival by the marginal peoples. Reversing these processes of resource destruction is, therefore, a precondition for the removal of poverty and for overcoming the dynamics of underdevelopment. Since the processes that make some people rich are ecologically related to the processes that make the poor poorer, a genuine restructuring of society cannot simply be content with adjustments associated with sharing financial benefits. To work at all, it must go deeper and seek honest and just ways of sharing the full material costs of development. A social restructuring that ensures peoples' survival must extend beyond a politics of distribution to a politics of production and resource use that is related to the life-sustaining cultures of marginalised sectors and to the ecological requirements of a sustainable resource base.

Resource Conflicts and the Role of the State
Exponents of an 'alternative model', however, seldom decide the course of development, particularly in the poor countries of the South. In most of these countries, those who hold State power choose the pattern of economic growth, sometimes 'guided' by technocrats trained abroad, by international financial pressures, and by the structures of the world capitalist economy. National military power and national prestige easily prevail over other goals which may threaten elite privileges or which fail to produce the symbols of modernity. The economic growth model based on modern technologies wins hands down most of the time, and even if the national elites seek a more viable approach, it is often threatened by interventionary pressures.

In a large number of countries of the South, the State assumes for itself or claims to assume the role of promoting development. But more often than not, State-sponsored development policies work against equity-oriented goals both in the short term and in the long run; they also willy-nilly become subservient to global interests. Theoretically, the emphasis on increasing productivity should benefit both small and large producers. However, those who have the capital resources to start with and have access to government loans necessarily possess a built-in advantage. Small and marginal farmers, for example, have no capital and have very limited access to credit because they have no collateral to guarantee the loans.

Once the State becomes the agent of development, it provides the political context for the transformation of the local commons into a series of global commodities. It does so both overtly and covertly. Changes are introduced in legislation that subtly erode entitlements of the poor. New subsidies, concessions and support prices create a background against which destructive changes in resource-utilisation occur. The State as the planner, financier, and executor of certain types of development strategies becomes both a participant and an adversary in conflicts over natural resources. Yet, the State also acts as arbiter in these conflicts. Politically, this dual role of the State as adversary and judge is leading to an ethos of resistance in the form of the emergence of peoples' interest groups that seek to enforce new types of social accountability. Ecology movements attempt to restructure the State in order to ensure that development plans and projects are not forced from the top by the State machinery but are created and shaped by local communities.

There is also a contradiction in the role of the State at the international plane. As a sovereign entity, the State alone has the power to control foreign interests within its domestic realm. Many Third World States, in fact, do exercise, or try to exercise, that power. However, those countries that have adopted the model of export-led growth, in close association with transnational corporations and banks, often find themselves buffeted by global market forces. The State is thus involved in conflicts over resources at the intra-State level as well as the inter-State level. There are revealing examples of contradictory tensions. For instance, the plunder of Brazil's Amazon basin by transnational forestry and cattle-ranching interests is not perceived by the Brazilian State as an encroachment on its sovereignty. However, the suggestion that international conservationists should advise Brazil on how to protect these precious Amazonian resources is at once perceived as an assault upon State-sovereignty.

It seems that while 'sovereignty' may be invoked when questions of 'national security' are at stake, it is quietly ignored when there is an international as well as domestic economic interest at work that affects the 'security' of natural resources. An unresolved tension between the 'security' of the State, basically its political power *vis-a-vis* the civil society and the 'security of natural resources', which is the basis for the biological and cultural survival of its subjects, links the process of militarisation with conflicts over natural resources. Most often, the issue is decided in favour of militarisation.

The developmental role of the socialist State falls in the second model we have described above. Socialist countries have sought, and to a considerable degree achieved, distributive justice to the producers. However, in these States too, particularly in Eastern Europe and the Soviet Union, resource-conflicts have appeared in recent times. Our analysis in the chapter on the global economic crisis shows that the conventional Marxist view on the role of science and technology and central planning was over-simplified. Marxist perspectives on 'productivity' and of 'growth' also omitted the costs of depletion of natural resources, and to that extent they were influenced by the Western intellectual heritage. The theoretical assumption that nature was inexhaustible, a supplier of 'free goods', underlies this failure to assess the ecological context of resource policy. Moreover, the socialist model of development prescribed the building of heavy industries for all socialist States, regardless of their resource situation, and without much sensitivity to the circumstances of local, impoverished peoples.

The immediate factors that drew attention to resource-conflicts in socialist States included rising energy prices, the impact of the global economic crisis, the change-over from 'extensive' to 'intensive' industrial development, as well as the demonstration effects of the Western 'consumer society'. But long-lasting degenerative changes had taken place even before these immediate causes had come into play. Extensive industrialisation had led to urbanisation with all its attendant problems. Agriculture had become more and more mechanised and its dependence on chemicals and high energy inputs had increased rapidly. Problems of human and natural ecology had, thus, been accumulating over the decades. More recently one can see these and similar problems over natural resources beginning to surface in the less developed socialist countries of East and South-East Asia. Despite this, the socialist development model has yet to devise a systematic and convincing way of combining economic growth with ecological stability.

Increasingly, in a world globally integrated at the top, the 'national security State' works towards creating insecurities for its people through threats to their ecological and cultural survival. The State, far from being a provider of security, has become a major source of insecurity for people. While the rhetoric of environmental protection grows, development policy in the Third World countries to colonise new regions and new elements of nature, undermining the security of life-support systems and livelihoods. This trend, set in motion by the State, has generated a counter-trend, the ecology movements of the people. They articulate meaningful concepts of security for all, including the future generations. And in doing so, they demonstrate that issues of peace and security are intimately linked to questions of maldevelopment, ecological degradation, abuse of human rights and loss of cultural identity.

Militarisation and Resource Conflicts

The contradiction between national security and the security of natural resources informs, to an extent far more than is generally realised, the conflicts between States, regardless of the development model adopted. National security, as currently conceived, demands an ever-increasing military build-up that diverts financial resources and human ingenuity away from the more basic needs. In the case of the less developed countries of the South, the military build-up diverts natural resources into the generation of financial resources, particularly foreign exchange, for purchases on the global arms market. The resulting export-oriented resource use runs into direct conflicts over natural sustenance-oriented natural resource use.

At another level, conflicts over natural resources create violence between groups, and resistance to and revolts against the State which, in turn, induce further militarisation of the State. In such cases, militarisation becomes a precondition for certain types of development; the 'national security State' and the 'national development State' are often two sides of the same coin. Only through the violent suppression of resource-conflicts can the State proceed with economic growth-oriented development. Such a relationship between resource-conflicts and militarisation is clearly visible in many parts of the South. The African continent, countries of the South and South East Asia and Latin America offer numerous examples of different variants of this relationship. Irrespective of whether there is a frankly acknowledged military regime or not, the State frequently resorts to armed suppression of resource-conflict.

So far we have discussed resource-conflicts within countries. These pertain to many basic resources for sustaining life. But there are also many other resources that are vital for industrial and military uses. Their quantities, their supply and demand patterns and levels of availability vary from country to country or region to region. These factors combine to generate competition over such resources among States. In the process of competition and conflict, alliances or winning coalitions may be formed among States in order to deny non-members a share in the resources and to maximise the members' access to them. The resolution of the political or military conflicts fought over resources results in specific configurations of power and structural arrangements. It is this structure of power that then produces a corresponding pattern of control over resources. Once established, such a control pattern must be sustained. Often, resort to physical, political, economic or psychological coercion becomes one way of lending legitimacy to an arrangement of this kind. The mode of producing goods and services (from resources) in any given society is monopolised by a privileged few, whether one society seeks the resources of another society or whether there are conflicts or competition over resources within a particular society.

In the context of the struggle for military power and the fact that military power itself is conceived in terms of weapons produced by modern technology, those materials that are strategically important have become the cause for many military conflicts between States. The importers of raw materials for industry and the military are basically the developed industrialised economies of Europe and North America. Although they possess many of the strategically important natural resources within their territories, they suffer from acute shortages of some others, e.g., petroleum, uranium, cobalt, copper, rubber etc. Given their high rate of dependence on such resources of the South and the role these resources can play with respect to their own military establishments and economies within the world, security of supply becomes an important dimension of geopolitics. Avoiding the loss of control over strategic resources provides a powerful rationale for militarised structures of power. Dr. Henry Kissinger put it succinctly during the historical showdown that was sparked off by the oil embargo of 1973 and 1974 when he said: "If the oil does not come, we go and get it". Any sign of the West going and getting 'it' would probably provoke a military response from the East, raising to intolerable levels risks of a general, possibly nuclear, war.

A militarised structure of power can be maintained through the presence of a striking force in or around the suppliers' territory and through the use of secret services for clandestine activities. Lower down the scale influencing political developments or putting economic pressure on the supplier is relied upon. In the last resort intervention to change the recalcitrant regime through force is relied upon. Several resource-rich countries of Africa and Latin America have had *coups d'etat*; some have experienced insurgencies engineered from abroad. These methods are, of course, adopted *vis-a-vis* independent States. In the case of a colonial situation, the use of direct military methods had been routinely practised. This is one reason why certain wars of independence by the people of Algeria, Kenya, Angola, Zimbabwe, Mozambique and the still raging wars in the Spanish Sahara and Namibia have been so prolonged. The same story is likely to repeat itself in the case of the resource-rich satellite countries in a neo-colonial situation. Strategic and resource interests have greatly complicated the situation in South Africa despite a massive global revulsion of public opinion (including in the United States and Western Europe) against the *status quo*.

Countries which seek to assert sovereignty over their natural resources in the face of interventionary pressures, soon discover that they are not strong enough to stand up to the formidable external structures of economic and military power that faces them. As a result, they are forced to seek the countervailing power of another alternative structure, thus ending up with compromised independence on one or the other side of the global Cold War.

Whether it is militarisation or ecologically destructive development policies—usually the two go together—human and cultural rights of the people become primary casualties. We have already discussed how threatened is the biological survival of tribal peoples, marginal subsistence-farmers and the farmers displaced by agribusiness. Africa is already in a condition where millions are being denied the right to live. While there are many other causes for these African tragedies, even agencies like the World Bank are now admitting that inappropriate development strategies and improper development priorities are at the root of the dangers to survival in Africa.

The Issue of Cultural Survival

Development policies which destroy resources or divert them from the needs of the poor to the greed of the rich deny fundamental human rights by threatening lives, livelihood and cultures. Unfortunately, in the prevalent fragmentary worldview the rights are regarded as separately related to ecological, economic and cultural aspects. People do not merely have a right to survive by access to resources that make life possible and access to work that provides entitlements to resources for sustenance. They have a fundamental right to living and working according to their own choice. They have a right to determine their lifestyles. Development aimed at global markets, global farms and global factories is erasing the rich cultural diversity of our planet, and also undermining the ecological base that has made this diversity such a valuable part of the human heritage. The modernising State is destroying peoples' life-support systems, their livelihoods and their cultures. Ecology movements throughout the world are offering resistance to such multiple violations of human rights that are the consequence of poor resource policies.

Ecological conflicts are at once cultural conflicts, not merely because natural resources form the material basis of cultural life, but also because ways of using natural resources are linked to values, both cognitive and ethical. At the broadest level, a colonising culture emerging from the modern West is running into conflict with all the diverse cultures of the world and with the sciences, technologies, production systems and rights that these cultures embody. The destruction of cultures goes on simultaneously at the material, cognitive and ethical levels. 'Ecocide' destroys the resource base on which diverse cultures survive and leads to 'ethnocide'. The genetic erosion in forests and farms has undermined the material basis of diverse traditions in food and medicine. Agribusiness and commercial forestry thus destroy cultures while they destroy resources. With the erosion of the base is linked the erosion of knowledge, of nature. Ecological perceptions of nature as living traditions are threatened with extinction because their material context is destroyed. And that is destroyed by a claimed superiority of a colonising and reductionist culture. Finally, at the deepest level, values of conservation which have guided most Third World peasant and forest cultures are being undermined even as the global rhetoric of conservation grows among those enjoying resource-wasting lifestyles. Gandhi's statement that the earth was enough for the needs of all but not for their greed was probably the most powerful summary of a political ideology which sees issues of conservation necessarily in relation to the issues of justice and peace.

The culture of resource destruction which is spreading through 'development' embodies a culture of violence—of violence not just against nature, but also violence in society. As resource destruction increases, resource-conflicts intensify, leading ultimately to the militarisation of civil society. Armed and violent conflicts between pastoralists and agriculturists in Africa and Asia, and between settlers and tribals in Latin America are examples of the emerging culture of violence even among groups which earlier had a symbiotic relationship. In most situations, however, since resource exploitation is indirect and non-local through the invisible chains we have spoken of earlier, and since the victims often share the development ideology, a shrinking resource base with shrinking livelihood opportunities translates into a pervasive culture of insecurity and loss of identity. It is this ecological and cultural insecurity which creates the context of the growing ethnic conflicts, particularly in regions which have had the most rapid and intensive development, and hence, the most drastic disruption of ecological and cultural patterns.

Environmental degradation, in the final analysis, is simultaneous cultural annihilation. The survival of the earth as a living system in all its diversity is the precondition for cultural plurality and the survival of indigenous cultures and ethnic minorities.

We have mostly spoken of the South. But in the North as well, thermal pollution, acid rain, the breakdown of the ultraviolet shield and the greenhouse effect are gradually endangering life-support systems and impinging on the rights of the people of the North. Their right to health is violated by low radiation, chemicalisation of the environment and the increasing disposal of pollutants and toxic wastes in the atmosphere, in inadequate dumping grounds and in water courses. Environmental degradation is denying people of the North the right to participate fully in the earth's resources, and is depriving future generations as well. The earth, being a common aggregate resource of humanity, establishes an ethos in which every inhabitant has as much right to its enjoyment as any other. This principle, axiomatic though it may seem, is being constantly undermined by technology at the command of the elites in industrialised nations as well as in the developing countries. Nations and communities lacking the technology, presuming that it is benign, are denied their share of what the planet has to offer. For example, the right to an equal share in the wealth of the sea is effectively negated by a technology which will help the most highly developed and capital-rich nations to exhaust seabed resources before the developing regions can ever reach them.

There is also a generational dimension to these concerns. The right to the earth's resources belongs not only to those who are alive now. Countless future generations should have as much right to these life-sustaining resources as past and present generations.

Since conflicts over natural resources are so closely intertwined with the issues of science and technology, ecology, development, economic well-being, militarisation, culture and a democratic political order, both domestic and international, it is not surprising that grassroot movements which initially espouse only a single cause find themselves sharing concerns and sensibilities when they happen to come together in settings of joint action. They discover that all of them seek peace with transformation, although each is responding to a specific cluster of problems immediately facing individuals and communities in its distinctive geographical, political, economic and social location. These local preoccupations make movements appear fragmented, transient, even parochial.

While grassroot movements have developed a powerful critique of the dangerous trends that are at work today, being often isolated from one another, they are unaware of the complex interlinkages that underlie their predicament. Hence the 'alternatives' they seek also generally appear to be *ad hoc* and disjointed remedial measures. The decision-makers whom they challenge can, thus, play one movement against another. Farmers uprooting Eucalyptus saplings can be pitted against workers in the wood-pulp industry. Peasants being displaced by a hydro-electric project can be pitted against urban consumers of electricity. Those protesting against diversion of resources to the military can be pitted against nationalists. And so on. It is crucial to avoid these traps and join forces—across boundaries that delimit seemingly distinct substantive concerns but are in fact manifestations of a single underlying reality.

Our effort in this chapter—as in this volume as a whole—has been to learn from the different struggles carried on by the victims of conflicts over natural resources. From such observation, a theory —and hopefully a programme of action—for transformation can emerge. The methods and goals of the movements in the South and in the North provide both tools and building blocks. Such a theory of ecologically sound development has to be based on creative forms of alternative thinking in the area of demilitarisation, political democracy, economic well-being and the basic rights of the peoples. Likewise, the programme of action for a liberating peace needs to rely upon the synergy of various efforts by the peoples of the West, the East, the North and the South.

5

Human Rights, Political Democracy and the Survival of Cultures

If there is one dimension of the human condition that seems deeply related with all others, and which on this account exhibits contradictory pulls, it is the dimension comprising human rights, political democracy, and the survival of cultures in the world today. Any interpretation of 'human rights' which does not take into account the contradictions in economic, social and political life will miss the distinctive quality of its reality. The most fundamental expression of this opposition is found in the fact that individuals and groups in various parts of the world are becoming increasingly aware that their experiences of deprivation and oppression are unnecessary and can be overcome by political action. On the other hand, leaders and public officials, responding especially to the dynamics of State-building, the imperatives of 'modernisation' and global tendencies toward militarisation, find it difficult to govern without reliance on an expanding apparatus of repression. And yet, in an encouraging number of instances, these leaders are also finding extreme repression to be a political and economic dead end. In this lies the whole dialectic of human rights.

It is noteworthy that all leaders endorse the ideals of human rights and political democracy. The numerous instances of defection from these ideals, often in the most extreme manner, have the inevitable effect on drawing into question the legitimacy of the governing process and reinforcing the moral, even the legal status of opposing and resisting activity. We live at a time when international law and the United Nations unambiguously endorse human rights, political democracy, and the rights to autonomy and the survival of cultures and ethnic groupings. No government can ignore these normative developments without, at the very least, losing respect before the world public opinion. At the same time, the struggle for these goals is largely being waged within the confines of the sovereign territorial State. There is only very minimal transnational implementing power and little political will to protect victims of abuse, even of the most gross form of abuse, and deliberate efforts to nullify the identity of peoples in whole or part. Nothing is more despicable in recent international history, for instance, than to turn ravaged Kampuchea into a geopolitical football by lending support to Pol Pot opposition forces, the worst perpetrators of genocide since Hitler, so as to resist the extension of Vietnamese, and indirectly, Soviet influence in the region. There is no doubt that superpower rivalries and quests for dominance stabilise repressive regimes from without and destabilise and frustrate certain political developments that are positive from the viewpoint of human rights and political democracy. The tenuous protection of human rights is largely a reflection of a wider character of international statecraft.

This fundamental and complex tension assumes a variety of forms reflecting variations in ideology; in the position and forms of the State in civil society; in respect of the connections with the world economy; and in terms of the great diversity of internal economic, social and cultural circumstances. Of particular concern, at this historical time, is the mounting pressure against a variety of indigenous peoples, who have been bypassed by the modernising and ethnic mainstream. They are being victimised in various ways, many so severe that their survival as a distinct people is being placed in jeopardy. What is striking about this very complex texture exhibiting such great variety is a pronounced overall condition of intensifying pressure on human rights, political democracy, and the survival of cultures under the unifying impact of certain global processes and structures. What seems evident, then, is a unifying impact of certain global processes and structures. As with the economic crisis, it is essential to comprehend specific national and sub-national pressures on human rights and political democracy by delineating certain structural characteristics that effectively limit the discretion of leaders and shape the unfolding role of the sovereign State in its relationship with the people. In order to increase understanding of these characteristics, we shall consider the *problematique* of human rights under the following rubrics:

1. a depiction of the basic dynamic trend towards deprivation and oppression, and the counter-trend towards struggle for the restoration of a certain measure of human rights and democracy;

2. State-building as a contributory factor;

3. capital formation patterns as a contributing factor;

4. interventionary diplomacy and geopolitical rivalry as a contributing factor;

5. the special phenomenon of the nuclear national security State;

6. political style as an outcome of overall process towards militarisation; and

7. positive prospects and alternative approaches.

The basic situation lends itself to neither optimism nor pessimism. There are many occasions for lament, but others for celebration, too. Ours is especially a historical period of struggle, between East and West, North and South. It is worthwhile to participate in this struggle to promote a more humane future at all levels of societal existence, from those of a community scale to that which embraces humanity as a whole, and extends concern even to the survival of the non-human environment.

Basic Trend

Despite the nominal adherence of virtually every government to a common framework of human rights and constitutional government, as embodied in the main international legal instruments, the overall cumulative tendency in every part of the world seems to be in the direction of deprivation and denial of basic human rights. There are exceptions, including reversals of severe crises of human rights (the elimination from power of such genocidal figures as Pol Pot in Kampuchea and Idi Amin in Uganda), moderating trends (the restoration of democracy in India after the Emergency, Argentina and Brazil), active and courageous struggles against repressive regimes (for instance, Chile and Poland), and notable long-term regimes (for instance, Chile and Poland), and notable long-term achievements (particularly in the establishment of constitutional government in the former fascist States of Germany, Italy and Japan). Yet, in every region, serious assaults on rights are taking place. This pattern can be categorised in very general terms.

In the Third World, there are very few governments that consistently uphold human rights and maintain the constitutional promises of their own legal systems. Explicit military rule has emerged in country after country in Asia, Africa, and Latin America. Even where the military does not assume the reins of government directly, militarised politics is widespread in the form of 'martial law' regimes, secured and prolonged over several years at a stretch, 'emergency powers' used to suspend normal constitutional rights, and the extension of executive control over other institutions of the State, and even over the organs of public opinion. It is notable that these repressive developments are evident in a very large number of countries, irrespective of whether the orientation of the regime is Left (socialist) or Right (capitalist). To be sure, this is not merely a reflection of domestic developments. One important source of generalised influence on Third World countries is exerted by the superpowers, or by other First World countries, affecting at once public policies and modes of governance, especially in regions treated as falling within spheres of influence. Democratising tendencies in Central America and the Caribbean are definitely opposed by superpower interventionary diplomacy. At the same time, militarisation has not generally worked out well with respect to economic development. These failures undermine the legitimising justifications for repression associated with 'discipline' and 'efficiency'. The property-owning classes become divided and a segment grows disenchanted with repression. The restoration of democracy in Argentina and the growth of urban opposition to Marcos in the Philippines are prominent illustrations. In cases where economic progress is impressive, as say in South Korea, the pressures to open the political process are associated with efforts to stabilise and legitimise the government at home and abroad, and avoid the kind of populist backlash that engulfed the Shah of Iran.

In the socialist world, a similar pattern is evident. The State group rights are exceedingly difficult to protect if threatened or denied. The ideology of a liberating socialist State mechanism (that is, entrusted to the vanguard of the proletariat) is inherently liberating for the society as a whole. Yet, in practice, a variety of societal resistances emerge and engender a coercive response by the State leadership. This pattern is by now so consistently in evidence as to be virtually synonymous with the adoption of socialism, at least within a Marxist-Leninist frame. Genuine counter-revolutionary pressures from within and without the socialist community of States reinforce and justify for policy-makers this pattern of denial, as when the socialist superpower grows concerned about tendencies in favour of liberal democracy within its orbit (Poland), or when defensive militarisation is a necessary security reaction to the threat of intervention from anti-socialist centres of State power (Nicaragua). In a very real sense, both superpowers make the emergence of governing structures that are sensitive to human rights and political democracy virtually impossible in closely aligned, subordinate countries. Whether intervention is successful or not, its effect on the affected society is a militarising one. Chilean militarisation came after the fall of Allende. And Cuban militarisation arose in part to guard the Cuban revolution against a genuine American threat, giving substance to anti-Castro exile activities.

But there is something more at work here, as well. It seems increasingly clear that anti-democratic forms of State socialism cannot be legitimised in socialist societies; political stability rests on continuous coercion. Such a posture is costly in economic and cultural terms. There is an increasing number of socialist critics of these repressive patterns who insist that only by allowing more democratising to take place can these countries achieve economic efficiency, political independence, social viability, and even the values associated with socialism. In this respect, the relative economic and political success of Hungary is correlated with its somewhat greater degree of internal freedom in the Kadar period since 1956.

In the First World, the pattern of erosion of human rights and political democracy is more subtle, and largely represents certain new developments arising out of the technological features of modernity.

In many First World countries there are serious human rights problem areas, especially of a collective character, arising in relation to marginal peoples (the poor, minorities), indigenous peoples who remain apart in non-industrialised enclaves or micro-politics (Indian nations and peoples in North America, Scandinavia or the 'tribal' peripheries in the low countries of Germany and Austria), and the large stream of migrants, refugees and Third Worlders. Of course, these problems are often less centrally visible because earlier deprivations had proceeded much further, in some instances achieving extinction, or virtual extinction.

Some special threats to human rights in the West are connected closely with the security role of the modern State, especially if the State projects its power beyond its own territory or possesses nuclear weaponry. Power projection involves a constant capability for, and disposition towards, intervention abroad; it puts the government of the intervening State in a position of denying central political and legal norms associated with respect for the sovereign rights of other societies. This normative friction usually generates some domestic opposition to intervention, encouraging secrecy and punishment of dissent. It has also given rise to extra-constitutional centres of authority, e.g., the Pentagon and the National Security Council in the United States, legitimised as extensions of the executive, but in reality grossly violating the 'balance' of constitutional government. In short, imperial geopolitics and human rights/political democracy are not compatible.

A related problem for the major First World countries arises from the direct or indirect (via alliances and collective security arrangements) possession of high technology weaponry, especially nuclear weapons. In theory, all modern States are supposed to be creatures of law and morality; to the extent that nuclear weaponry and the doctrines governing its use are incompatible with these norms of restraint, there is a basic infringement of the rights of citizens to be morally and legally governed. On a different plane, minimal rights of participation in the overall process of governance are at stake. Recourse to war becomes a matter beyond any effective political control.

The Formation of Modern States

State-building in the present period has exerted great pressure on commitments to human rights and political democracy, and have endangered numerous cultural and ethnic identities that have stood in the way of this centralising and modernising momentum. As with other aspects, the overall situation is extremely uneven as between different regional and national circumstances, and yet there is also evident a generalised global pattern. We do recognise that the modern State has performed certain crucial liberatory roles, overcoming the disarray of unorganised societal life, setting normative standards to overcome cruel, even barbaric local and provincial practices, and strengthening the capabilities of hundreds of millions of formerly colonised people to assume control over their own political destiny. Without effective State mechanism, societal life might well become intolerable, a virtually permanent civil war of faction contra faction (e.g., Lebanon), as well as extreme vulnerability to penetration and manipulation from the outside.

At the same time, the State as the central coercive mechanism in relation to societal forces has produced a variety of repressive arrangements. For one thing, States are often artificially constituted political and legal domains that do not correspond in their boundaries to natural communities or felt identities. This lack of correlation is especially evident in contemporary Africa and portions of Asia where the State boundaries were arbitrarily superimposed by colonial arrangements on diverse ethnic and cultural communities. The colonising State provided a level of authority that stood outside and above contending internal elements. These elements coalesced in many circumstances to struggle against the exploitative and alien character of the colonial arrangement and on behalf of sovereign independence. After independence, however, the anguish of State-building included the outbreak of often intense inter-ethnic and inter-religious rivalries relating to political and economic power, cultural prestige, and control over territory and resources.

To begin with, it was difficult in the post-independence period to sustain a balanced coalition among the diverse tribal, ethnic, religious, and cultural elements. Most States were in this sense multinational or multi-tribal, but the governmental authority was generally dominated by one or two of these constituent elements, others being excluded altogether or discriminated against. Especially smaller and weaker collective identities were crushed or marginalised. Indigenous peoples with no transnational visibility and no experience in modern political life were all the more vulnerable. Maintenance of these one-sided States depended on coercion and this invited resistance and induced the militarisation of political life across the full range of State-society relations.

These tendencies have of late acquired highly volatile forms as patterns of domination and mechanistic calculations of numerical strength have paved the way for the State to subject ethnic, religious and linguistic minorities to intense repression, at times verging on genocide. The fate of the Sikhs in India, Tamils in Sri Lanka, the Kurds in the Middle East, the Eritreans in Ethiopia, the Basques in Spain and the Chinese in Indonesia and Vietnam are leading examples of State repression. More subtle forms of discrimination exist in Malaysia against the Chinese, in Indonesia against the Sumatrans, in India against the Muslims and generally against the vast peripheries of social (as distinct from religious) minorities like the tribals, the 'untouchables' and 'backward classes' most of whom also happen to be poor and whose centuries old resource base has been eroded under the impact of capitalist development.

These problematic circumstances were aggravated by the infatuation of most governing elites with a modernising image of development that would be facilitated by effective political centralisation on the one hand and economic discrimination on the other, i.e., by devoting disproportionate resources and energies to those regions and elites most able to register rapid progress as measured by the criteria of industrialisation, economic growth, and urbanisation. This biasing of State-building was reinforced by the activities of international financial institutions, or overall development thinking by Western-educated technocrats. In sum, two distinct, yet mutually reinforcing, tendencies have been evident: first of all, the efforts by the nationalist inheritors of colonial administration to consolidate State power in the face of internal political forces pushing for access to power or towards varying forms of autonomy; and secondly, the developmental worldview dominating the outlook of these State-building elites that looked askance especially at 'backward' peoples and regions and focusses efforts on those generally more urban groups with shared ideological and ethnic affinities.

The Colonial Powers along with the United States and the Soviet Union provided models of power and economic development as a consequence of rapid industrialisation and the capacity to rely upon technological innovation to assure societal progress. One difficulty with extending this development model to the Third World was that it was adopted uncritically and transplanted without due regard for societal contexts that were relatively far more homogeneous; the industrial countries had a lot of time available for coping with the turmoil associated with industrial growth and had access to colonial lands for both cheap raw materials and markets—including *lebensraum* for their surplus populations. There was little understanding of this either among the leaders who came to occupy positions in the 'new States' or among the specialists from abroad who provided privileged advice to them.

Many Third World leaders—and their advisors—regarded State-building and development (conceived essentially as economic growth) to be the highest of political priorities. With such a conception of priorities, tribal peoples resistant to modernisation were treated as impediments to be swept aside for the greater good. Moreover, growth dynamics were generally given precedence over redistributive efforts to alleviate poverty, and even more so, over conservationist and environmental concerns. In effect, the logic of the modernising State tended to validate the neglect of basic human needs for the majority of its people, and to intervene in a reactive fashion in various struggles over the allocation of natural resources. This kind of State measured success by growth, and thus tended to give multinational corporations and banks a comfortable home and to concentrate capital investments on projects that did not benefit the bulk of the population much, if at all. "Brazil is doing well, but its people are not", was an apt comment by one of the country's leading technocrats during a peak moment in growth-led and highly militarised developmentalism.

This State-building juggernaut was also reinforced by the failure of most intellectuals in the Third World to appreciate the importance of civil liberties and restraints on government. Those Marxists who harboured apolitical perspectives on the relationship between liberty and liberation viewed constitutional concerns as 'bourgeois' preoccupation that withdrew energy from the central drama of class struggle. Even non-Marxists regarded the urgencies of poverty and development as the over-riding public concerns, even if they implied some repressive policies. In this regard there has been a genuine reassessment of positions. The many abrogations of constitutional order in the Third World which permitted regimes of oppression have created a genuine appreciation of the liberal framework which restrains governments, in most instances, by respect for the inalienable rights of its citizens. The Indian 'Emergency' of 1975 was a crucial learning experience in this regard. State-building as a justification for repressive power, that is, at the expense of personal freedom and political democracy, was definitely regressive for the people as a whole, in fact more for the poor and the exploited than for urban intellectuals. In all countries, no matter how serious their level of societal distress, there was neither necessity nor justification for shutting down rights. Furthermore, the record shows no sustainable efficiencies associated with such repression. The Southern Cone countries in South America turned from democracy and human rights in the decade between the mid-1960s and to the mid-1970s, in part to 'discipline' the economy. The economic results were so disappointing that save Chile, where the Pinochet regime is holding on to the reins by brutal police methods in the face of a shrinking power base, democracy has been substantially restored, partly to revive the economy! In the Philippines, also, economic revival is now associated by even the majority of business leaders with establishing a more humane and consensual relationship of the government to the people; their support was important for overthrowing the Marcos regime.

There are important differences in outlook and performance between capitalist-oriented and socialist-oriented governments. By and large, capitalist-oriented societies, even if politically and economically repressive, have displayed considerable tolerance for individual economic initiatives and provide a greater range of consumer and career choices. For instance, in many countries pursuing a strong anti-communist line at the State and market levels, intellectual life continues to be heavily influenced by Marxist thought. Furthermore, the bourgeois values entrenched in the society are positively connected with cultural vitality in a manner that achieves greater independence even in an otherwise anti-democratic political order.

In contrast, socialist-oriented societies, even if politically and culturally repressive, have embodied a serious commitment to realise basic human needs of their people as a whole and to cut disparities based on class differences and traditional land tenure patterns. China, Cuba, North Korea, and Vietnam are illustrative in the Third World, while the countries of Eastern Europe characterise the socialist world. In these countries the State predominates to a great extent, as market forces have been severely weakened, often virtually eliminated, and cultural activities are regarded as exclusively serving State and Party positions. There are variations, of course, in both patterns, but the generalisations seem accurate for purposes of interpreting overall trends.

It is possible to generalise still further by distinguishing between the commitment of bourgeois ideologies to individual rights and of Marxist ideologies to collective rights. But in foreign policy, both orientations appear selective and hypocritical. Each favours self-determination, human rights, and full sovereignty for States within the geopolitical orbit of the other. The Soviet Union supports these goals for the peoples of Central America, while obstructing their achievement in East Europe and Afghanistan. Washington applauds Solidarity in Poland and dissent in the Soviet Union, while it supports and stabilises some of the most repressive regimes in the world that are Western-oriented.

It is unfortunate that the two main styles of State-building in the Third World—capitalist and socialist—have both proved rather repressive of indigenous cultural identities. This insensitivity has been accentuated by two converging preoccupations. One is the preoccupation with achieving technological prowess; for achieving that goal homogenising local diversities (if need be, by force) and subjecting the entire societies to the dictates of technocrats and managers are considered absolutely necessary although the process clearly undermines political freedoms. The second is the preoccupation of the modern State with its identity as a war machine. This conception encourages the acquisition of modern military capabilities and, over time, causes a subtle shift in the civilian/military balance within the bureaucratic structure. As the most modernised sector of a State that cherishes modernisation, the military tends to predominate in policy-making councils and reinforces technocratic hold over society. This does not require literal and overt military leadership. As soon as a militarist outlook towards the management of conflict, whether internal or external, emerges, oppressive consequences ensue. Coercive strategies are preferred, and the militarised sector spills over into the redesign and deployment of, for example, the police along modern para-military lines. Many Third World cities that have only the most primitive technologies for the provision of basic services, have elaborate computerised surveillance systems administered by the police. That is, the fusion of modernisation and militarisation shape the quality of societal development, often at the expense of basic human needs and human rights.

These various State-building patterns have been reinforced by certain international economic processes. This pattern is perhaps, best studied in relation to the Pacific Rim NICs (newly industrialised countries). Transnational business and financial actors generally prefer to operate in States where societal forces, including labour, are adequately 'disciplined'. The superpowers, on the basis of their own experiences of State-building, have encouraged centralised growth-oriented development patterns in the Third World, and have pushed arms and military training both to increase trade and foreign exchange earnings, and to assure continuing influence. That is, the militarising potential of State-building has been definitely promoted by the overall geopolitical setting, including the rivalry of opposed Power blocs.

Capital Formation

We have already referred to the experience of the Southern Cone countries of Latin America. But there are others too, especially in Southeast Asia and generally the so-called NICs, which exhibit the same characteristics. Part of the justification for repressive policies among all these countries has been to eliminate the friction caused by labour unrest and political opposition. The underlying belief is that if wages are kept low and unrest disallowed, the investment climate would lead to a more robust industrial sector, more favourable conditions for the growth of competitive exports, and a stronger overall economy. In fact, a State-society tension arose in all these cases because only a small proportion of the potential workforce, and hence population, could benefit from such export-led growth models. Also, this marginalisation of working peoples was occurring in the face of growing political consciousness on the part of the masses and in religious institutions. The result was opposition and dissent, often in radical forms. Subsequently, the pressure on governments to neutralise these by harsh means was great.

The balance sheet here may, of course, be mixed. Some experiments in militarisation of the society have clearly failed, and a dynamic demilitarisation is occurring in some countries e.g., Brazil, Argentina, possibly Turkey. In other instances, economic growth has been kept up, as in the Pacific Rim countries, and only after achieving a measure of sustained growth have there been pressures for liberalisation, as well as towards incorporating an increasing share of the society in the growth dynamic. These are countries with relatively high levels of education, skilled manpower, strong US backing, and relatively equitable land tenure patterns simultaneously with the capacity to institutionalise regimes of repression. South Korea, Taiwan and Singapore might be the best current examples. There prosperity and even equity are guaranteed in return for accepting such regimes. There is resistance all right, sometimes within the ruling elite itself, but this is ruthlessly put down.

The main point is that policies relating to capital formation at various stages are used to legitimise curbs on human rights and political democracy. One important setting here has to do with the interaction between Third World governments and the International Monetary Fund (IMF). If IMF conditions for loans require a government to cut back on services to the poor, especially on food subsidies, and on the right of the working class to organise itself, the resulting unrest can be swift and violent and so can be the repressiveness of the government seeking to maintain requisite order in a situation of declining popular support. A vicious cycle indeed. But more vicious for the mass of the people than for any privileged classes.

Interventionary Diplomacy

Different from the economic rationale, though often operationally related to it, is the use of both overt and covert intervention by the metropolitan Powers. This too has been stoutly defended and provided with a theoretical and/or ideological justification. Thus, to rationalise support for covert operations to destabilise Allende's Chile, Henry Kissinger, then Secretary of State, made that extraordinary remark that is quoted often: "I don't see why we need to stand by and watch a country go communist due to the irresponsibility of its own people". Even leaving aside the misleading implication that Allende's leadership is equated with communist rule, Kissinger's statement reveals the contempt of a great Power for the exercise of political democracy by a subordinate State. Considerations of ideological alignment and geopolitical rivalry clearly take precedence in the way superpowers deal with the internal politics of Third World countries. Often, the consequence of these priorities is intervention in foreign societies in ways that sustain, aggravate, and even invent and institute patterns of repression. Patterns of intervention so motivated usually go against the flow of nationalism in the country concerned. This fact requires very high levels of coercion that are only possible by outsiders instituting puppet regimes and bolster them with money and arms over long periods of time.

Of course, some outside Powers in theory propagate human rights. The United States, for instance, claims to be using its diplomatic influence and economic presence in South Africa to promote reforms and lessen the rigours of *apartheid*. It is useful to compare the benign neglect of 'constructive engagement' (President Reagan's stance towards South Africa) with military intervention in the Caribbean/Central America region to eliminate from power governments with socialist leanings and alignments. In the former case, economic and geographical interests tend to overwhelm whatever concern exists about an admittedly abhorrent pattern of governing that is dependent upon a daily and systematic repudiation of human rights for the great majority of the population. In the latter, rather promising experiments (e.g., Cuba, Nicaragua) in socialist developments are perceived and treated as geopolitical and economic threats that must be removed by covert means and non-military pressures if possible and by armed attacks if necessary.

Soviet patterns of diplomacy are rather similar in their spheres of influence. The disposition towards political democracy in Poland during the last several years has been stymied by Soviet threats of intervention and manipulation of Polish elites, including pressures that led to the installlation of a military officer as the head of the State for the first time in an East European country. Earlier interventions into Hungary (1956) and Czechoslovakia (1968) were examples of Soviet power management that curbed strong local urges towards more open forms of political democracy in these countries.

In addition to focussing on the obvious impact of foreign intervention on human rights, there is a need to discuss the problem of small States in the world and their vulnerability to a take-over, indirect or direct, by outsiders, either physically or in other ways. Lebanon and Cambodia are important examples of this. Both countries were victimised by their proximity to conflict among stronger neighbours. In both instances, the conflict spilled across their borders, disturbed the delicate domestic political arrangements, and produced tragic prolonged ordeals for the peoples involved. To sustain human rights in the world of today requires a capacity to uphold the sovereign rights of the State, not against all outsiders, but to a significant degree.

There are three further threats to human rights, political democracy and survival of cultures that call for special attention at this stage.

1. The threat posed by cultural chauvinism or religious bigotry is not sufficiently emphasised in human rights settings. The Iranian export of fundamentalist Islam is illustrated both in relation to certain positive impact and to the serious problems that followed. Khomeini's Islam is basically anti-colonial and anti-capitalist but it is also culturally stifling, intolerant of diversity and completely repressive towards women. Any form of fundamentalism can be

dangerous to these values, as was the anti-Sikh response to the assasination of Indira Gandhi, an orientation alien to mainstream Hinduism but one that, at least in the immediate aftermath of the assasination, got widespread support among the Hindus.

2. Human rights face the twin threat of rampant and corrosive communication media, modelled after and transferred from the First World, and other authoritarian indigenous communications policies that use foreign domination as a pretext for exerting often a more deadening and insidious control over citizens. In brief, we should begin to examine the politics of the new international communication order which would be biased in favour of modernising regimes and assess its possible impact on the survival of cultures as a human rights problem area. The issues are not simply those of domination of news-flows by transnational media but also of the monopoly of indigenous governments over local news-flows, often reinforcing each other in the form of a new international framework of control and manipulation—above all, of the mind.

3. Then there is the continuing threat to the world's intellectual community as reflected most urgently by the rising phenomenon of intellectual refugees. We must examine the common features of this phenomenon across political and economic systems that lead to State repression of intellectual activities and identify more clearly the best ways to attain and protect intellectual freedom. By its very nature, the departure of intellectual refugees from repressive regimes contributes to the 'brain drain' problem which raises the spectre of 'perverse incentives' for intellectuals to abandon their own societies. Often the intellectual portion of a society is virtually wiped out, either by emigration or by internal silencing (in effect, a stationary brain drain), not to speak of massive genocide of intellectual movements, as of the communists in Indonesia, or the more subtle but no less stifling persecutions of dissenting intelligentsia.

Nuclear National Security State
In general, the modern State has grown more militarised, especially as high technology has become an aspect of effective internal governance and as the speed and devastating effect of weaponry has required permament readiness for war. Militarisation works against

political democracy, human rights, and the survival of cultures. It emphasises the role of force in human affairs, and tends to view struggle as 'anti-national', especially in relation to marginalised peoples within and without the State. In these crucial respects, demilitarisation is the essential constructive perspective for protecting positive political values.

Some severe threats to human rights in the North are distinctively connected with the role and character of the modern State, especially of the superpowers. The processes of militarisation have tended to erode boundaries between peace and war. There is a constant danger of nuclear war, and an associated need to be always mobilised to fight such a war. To sustain this condition of perpetual readiness involves building an intelligence apparatus that generates abuses of human rights at home and abroad. It also establishes a *permanent emergency* that justifies secrecy and surveillance. In political theory, every State is a creature of law and morality; it is supposed to be subordinate to societal will. Nuclear weaponry and doctrines governing its uses are generally incompatible with these ideas, posing a potential crisis in the State-society relations. There is, thus, a basic infringement of the right of citizens to be morally and legally governed.

On a different plane, meaningful rights of participation in the overall process of governance are at stake in political democracies. To the extent national security policy is formed in secret counsels, away from standards of guidance or procedures of accountability, the leaders are free to act as they wish. For countries tied into alliance relations, or even for those opting for neutrality, this abridgement of constitutional order is particularly dramatic—the country leading the alliance can initiate nuclear war at the time and place of its choosing, with possibly apocalyptic results for countries other than itself. For citizens of the country that is the alliance leader, their own survival has been linked to a willingness to accept devastation as the possible price of protecting an ally under attack. No consent of the governed in any adequate respect has been given for these broad implications of modern alliance relations, or for the concrete enactment of such policies at a time of crisis.

The nuclear national security State also encroaches on democratic rights in another basic sense. The basic ideas of separation of powers, and checks and balances have been substantially nullified as the executive branch has obtained unconditional authority over occasions on which nuclear weapons are threatened or used. Furthermore, highly influential sectors of the bureaucracy with control over national security policy have evolved as largely autonomous actors in the polity, constraining media, public opinion and politicians through the control of information and oligopolistic control over experts. In these circumstances, electoral challenges are rendered almost meaningless, and the institutions of representative government are subordinated. In effect, when it comes to nuclear national security, no matter how liberal the formal political framework, the citizenry has been effectively disenfranchised.

The embodiment of military power in 'the invisible government' of the national security bureaucracy poses a very severe threat, and yet it is not generally experienced as such, even by 'the Opposition'. Other more superficial threats associated with 'policy', rather than 'structure', receive most of the attention. The reality of these deeper forms of opposition are disguised behind the formalistic trapping of democratic procedure. Yet the reality of preparing to fight nuclear wars without obtaining consent from the governed, or assuring the informed participation of allied or neutral third parties, represents basic denial of democratic prerogatives in the most crucial sphere of civic life. It also represents a continuing encroachment upon human rights associated with peace and survival, as well as the effective abridgement of sovereign rights for those third countries that would be affected by either the use of nuclear weapons or by the dynamics of the nuclear arms race.

As indicated at the outset of this section, demilitarisation is the essential dynamic to offset these developments. In the specific context of nuclearism, there is the more specific counter-dynamic of denuclearisation. Here, we have in mind those forms of nuclear arms control and disarmament that focus on nuclear weapons and work towards their reduction and elimination. In this regard, the renunciation of the nuclear option in the form of No First Use Declaration would seem like one constructive step, a step taken with considerable diplomatic emphasis by China and then the Soviet Union. But it is not necessarily helpful, if in exchange it leads to a build-up of conventional weaponry and a lowering of the overall firebreak between peace and strategic warfare. The Western nuclear powers have refrained from renouncing first-use options, seeking to retain the deterrence advantages associated with ambiguity about use. Denuclearisation is intertwined with other dimensions of the world situation. To reduce nuclearism while increasing militarism (the pressure by the militarised State to compensate) may end up increasing the risk of nuclear war, by lowering the thresholds of conventional war and leading to a situation in which the losing side resorts to nuclear weapons to reverse the tide of battle or to avoid defeat.

Political Style
The modernised or modernising State, with its strong technocratic dimension and its essentially militarised approach towards internal and external law-and-order challenges, tends to require a type of leadership that is not sensitive to claims put forward on behalf of human rights, political democracy and cultural survival. Priorities are constantly weighted in favour of technocratic considerations, including subordination of internal social policy to externally evolved standards set down by international financial institutions and foreign banks. 'The debt trap' ensures that leaders are considerably constrained in their capacity to direct State investment policy into channels that contribute to the satisfaction of basic human needs, to the protection of non-material dimensions of the civilisational patrimony that cannot easily be evaluated in monetary terms, or to the enhancement of the life-chances of marginalised peoples or sectors of population, for example, by taking adequate steps to uphold environmental quality, the basic cultural heritage, and the specific identities of minority or marginal cultures. These elements of societal well-being are neither well-represented within the State, nor are they generally able to exert effective pressure upon it.

If the sense of grievance grows, especially if the leadership is tainted with suspicions of large-scale corruption, then active resistance is likely to grow and assume extra-legal, illegal and even desperate forms. This dynamic encourages repressive responses, and a basic pattern for Third World State-society relations is established.

One widespread tendency in the face of this situation is to find effective means to depoliticise the society as a whole, via control of media and education, as well as by severely restricting activities of the legal Oppositon via harassment, denial of rights to hold meetings and demonstrations, and arrest and intimidation of dissenting politicians, journalists, and intellectuals. Such a process of depoliticisation is characteristic of virtually all parts of the world system, with the limited exception of Western Europe and isolated instances. It exists in the latter too, only the form is different. For instance, reliance on technocratic decision-making and on experts, lobbying on behalf of defence industries and high-tech development, and the use of classified information are among the ways the modern State proceeds even in the North. That has its serious consequences for the citizen's rights.

Positive Prospects and Alternative Approaches

The basic culminative trends are apparently unfavourable. We, however, feel that countertrends might gather strength in the years ahead, enabling a more encouraging assessment. State-building persists in a variety of modernising forms that neglect the rights of individuals and groups. The modern State, separated from the people as a whole and from marginalised or entrapped cultures and nations (the 'Third World' within and without, including minorities and indigenous peoples in the First World), has generally adopted a technocratic mode that relies on militarised governance. This apparatus of State power is used to control dissent and to demobilise, if not directly repress, societal forces. Fortunately, there are hope-inspiring counter-tendencies at work.

Increasing efforts are underway to establish non-governmental organisations for the protection of human rights and ethnic and cultural identities. These organisations are able to gather information, rally public opinion, embarass many State leaders, and intervene in repressive processes. Although often hampered by shortages of financial resources, and dependent on the cooperation of States or inter-State bodies for access to evidence, these transnational initiatives are giving individual and group victims of abuse a means to exert some counter-leverage. In instances of severe repression,

Human Rights

or in contexts where the victims lack the means to call attention to their plight, such initiatives are not very effective. And yet, overall, these initiatives, which are now being complemented by regional and sub-regional efforts, and indeed wholly indigenous movements, contain real promise for the future.

India provides a case where formal freedoms have been put to great use by non-State, non-Party actors and movements to counter repressive State agencies, chauvinistic attitudes among the middle classes, lumpenised infrastructures of crime and violence that usually flex their muscles on behalf of the upper classes, and the incipient brutalisation and militarisation (and 'para-militarisation') of the governing structures. Though still highly fragmented and diffuse, and riven by sectarian tendencies and individual egos masked as ideological differences, these activist organisations and 'movements' e.g., of ecology, women, the landless, the ethnic minorities, peace, provide a basic challenge to the State and often succeed in restraining its excesses. Similar tendencies are found in parts of Latin America and Southeast Asia.

Perhaps, more significantly, there are objective trends at work which are likely to assist these counter-cultural initiatives. The efforts to transform the State into an engine of modernising growth, even if the side-effect is to shut down the political process, has encountered serious obstacles. Self-proclaimed arguments about disciplined development have lost credibility as an overall justification for repression. In Southern Cone countries where repression was explicitly justified in these terms, high rates of inflation and unemployment, disappointing expansion of trade, large debt burdens, and general economic stagnation have generated a severe reaction that includes even the previously acquiescent, if not supportive, professional and business classes. Chile and the Philippines are two countries in which the new development ethos of technocratic dominance had to be fused with militarisation and repression of political life, following disastrous economic performance by these regimes. It is true that other repressive regimes such as in South Korea and Taiwan have fared somewhat better during the recent period despite difficult world economic conditions. But in these countries, too, the necessity for repression is being challenged, partly on the grounds that favourable economic performance would be enhanced by creating conditions more conducive to democratic and humane patterns of governance. In all instances, by now, developmental experiments have been sufficiently drawn into question largely on economic grounds themselves to stiffen resistance to encroachments on human rights and political democracy, and to alter the balance of intra-societal forces significantly in favour of a more positive and humane set of State-society relationship.

Similarly, in the advanced country context of the industrialised world, there is a growing appreciation of the dangers of war arising out of the militarisation of inter-State relations and of the need to evolve new forms of societal activism so as to exert greater democratic control over foreign policy. In this respect, the peace movements in Western Europe, North America, Australia and Japan have emerged to strengthen *direct* societal pressures on political leaders, partly as a result of the inability of representative institutions and procedures to be a vehicle of societal pressure. These movements, quite diverse from one another, have managed to enlist significant participation from the professional strata and from mainstream cultural and media groups.

Many independent new organisations have been formed, partly to express a loss of confidence in the manner in which the State is upholding security for the overall society. This loss of confidence is sharply accentuated by stands taken by established religious institutions that throw considerable doubt upon the propriety, prudence and legitimacy of State policy in the context of national security. The Catholic Church's Pastoral Letter in the United States on nuclear weapons is only one of a number of examples of religious backing for rather fundamental societal challenges directed at official policies. Church support for radical human rights, women's and other movements is also on the increase, despite occasional setbacks, and doctrinal disputes. Small stirrings of reaction against oppression and militarisation within other religious traditions are also in evidence (in the Middle East, in South Asia, in Africa) though these have to contend with obscurantist and chauvinistic tendencies among the same traditions.

There are other optimistic tendencies as well. Popular concerns about intervention in foreign societies create some resistance to militarisation within the State and across State boundaries. Pressures to reduce the size of defence spending relate closely to struggles over the use and allocation of financial and natural resources and to the societal control over the evolution of science and technology. Basic questions on the relationship between modern science and violence are being raised. Though spurred by the militarist virus overtaking the world, these questions go beyond militarism into the fundamentals of human freedom.

Beyond this, there is an emerging 'non-party political process' that is attempting to work out local and grassroot solutions for problems that had previously been left to the State, including provision of basic human needs, environmental protection, and the defence of indigenous peoples and non-modern cultures and ethnic groupings as well as vulnerable sections like the women and children, rendered more vulnerable when pushed to the edge of a computerised and militarised future. This informal political network of actors is, as yet, barely mapped, but its potential significance is profound. It holds out the promise of greatly expanding spaces within the civil society and of establishing greater societal control over the State through initiating a variety of initiatives designed to encourage the revitalisation of the democratic process, to defend the rights of indigenous peoples and threatened minority cultures, and to decentralise the institutions of the State.

And as all this happens, the thrust and perspective of the human rights movement expands to cover the hitherto neglected elements of human existence. With this the notion of rights is acquiring greater depth and comprehension. The old dichotomy between legal-political and socio-economic rights, between civil liberties and democratic rights, is coming to an end. Indeed, protection of the rights of the deprived and the dispossessed has come to occupy the centre of the human rights scene today. But it is more than just this transformation from the humanitarian compassion to a political assertion of the rights of individuals and classes and cultures of those who happen to have become victims of history. The human rights movement has extended in other ways too. For instance, in joining the concerns of civil liberties and democratic rights of the poor with those of the environment movement and the struggle over the resource base of the people, the human rights movement has not only deepened its philosophical and cultural moorings—beyond the early progressivist credo—but it has also acquired a planetary and extra-species sensitivity. And in throwing its weight behind the women's issue it has created a process of redefining both the content of politics and the nature of what constitutes 'politics'. The whole shift from the split between the personal and the political to the consciousness that 'personal is political' to the still deeper realisation that 'political is personal' represents a transformation in our thinking on political and ethical issues that has been spurred by the feminist movement. So is that movement's redefinition of the concepts of violence and peace, aggression and war, its capacity to transcend gender as such, and its basic revelation of the interrelatedness of life and existence. The same is the case when concerns of human rights, cultural survival, ecological prudence and feminist values join *inter se* and with the challenge of peace as posed by the peace movements.

Increasingly, these 'single-constituency' movements will be forced to find not just a common future and stake but the fact of their being one movement. Once this happens, it will provide a framework in which it is possible to extend the realm of individual liberty to the whole of human liberation. It is this ever deepening and ever enlarging conception of 'democracy' that will provide the basis of a resolution of the contradictory pulls we have noticed in this chapter.

6

Conclusion: Transforming the State

Those of us who have undertaken to study the *problematique* of peace with transformation are seriously disillusioned with the current state of social scientific thinking. We began with a conviction that the present fragmentation of social science theory into separate fields of study and separate disciplines was based on a set of past generalisations, past forms of classification and categorisation, past stories, that may not be relevant to, and indeed may hinder an understanding of, the present global crisis. We also rejected the universalist claim for social scientific theory, the notion that there is one story, one explanation for a particular phenomenon, such as the arms race or the economic crisis, and that identification of such an explanation can yield a solution. We started, instead, from the assumption that there are myriads of competing or conflicting explanations for phenomena or events and that the task of the social analyst is to develop an interpretation that provides an opportunity for constructive action in a given time and space. Yet, even if action were our only criterion for knowledge, an insistence on a single cause explanation would not necessarily be helpful. It is not very useful to identify the cause of the arms race as the military-industrial complex. Besides, it is misleading because the arms race can only be explained plausibly in several complementary ways.

Because we are ourselves—economists, lawyers, political scientists—prisoners of existing social scientific theory, we began our investigation by emphasising some interlinkages between existing fields of study. We identified four different dimensions of the global crisis, which were defined according to established traditions in social science—military, economic, ecological and socio-cultural. But our initial concern was to go beyond our own experience by investigating interlinkages between these dimensions. Moreover, we were not so much concerned with seeking one explanation for the crisis or to identify the problems of each dimension. Since we regard the crisis as multidimensional, our concern was to understand the contradictory ways in which the crisis in each dimension impinges on the crisis in other dimensions.

The accompanying matrix arises out of our methodology and summarises our preliminary findings. By expressing each dimension as a column and a row, we were encouraged to formulate interlinkages between each dimension and the others. The blank spaces in the diagonal are the uni-dimensional fields of conventional social science theory. The matrix does not express a deterministic view of the world. Rather it expresses an interpretation of crisis as the interplay of risk and opportunity. Above the diagonal we have summarised dangerous trends in each interlinkage, climaxing with the possibility of war or mass ecological or economic catastrophe. Below the diagonal we have summarised counter trends—some countervailing forces and actors that could lessen the dangers and could contribute to peace and global transformation.

For example, as our analysis of the four dimensions in this volume shows, the growth of militarisation has led to economic crises at the global as well as national and regional levels. Global military expenditure has been a contributory cause of the slow-down in capital accumulation processes in rich countries. In the Third World, the need to build up surpluses to enable the import of expensive and sophisticated weapons-systems has been keeping millions of people below the line of destitution quite unnecessarily. Militarisation and concomitant patterns of 'development' are also dictating priorities in the extraction and use of natural resources at the cost of denying to millions of people all over the world not only a decent minimum livelihood but access to sufficient stocks of renewable resources—forests, water, herbs, indigenous fruits and vegetables —supplies of which had often been previously sufficient. The culture

Conclusion: Transforming the State

of militarisation has not only spread war-psychosis among the people but it has also encouraged routine use of repressive violence; a tremendous growth of paramilitary forces to deal with socio-cultural problems has been taking place in recent years, particularly in the Third World. Military research and development has achieved such a high priority for most countries that it has distorted priorities in scientific research. Worst of all 'national security' systems have come to assume an autonomous character even in peacetime, and these have had a demoralising effect on public activity, often effectively usurping democratic rights and procedures, diminishing the power of the people to control their own governing process.

Yet counter-trends are also at work. Since the governments seem incapable of rising above their self-defined national and security interests, people have spontaneously taken to organising themselves in the form of peace-movements, particularly in the developed countries of the West. In the East as well as in the South, the issue of anti-militarisation is a constant feature of the movements against repression, inappropriate 'development' and ecological destruction, and is also a feature of movements for democratic rights in military-ruled and militarised single party-ruled States.

The global economic crisis and its impact on national economies has, in its turn, also contributed to the growth of militarisation. Political dissent arising out of economic distress is being frequently dealt with by the State through armed repression. The economic crisis, as our analysis shows, is also linked to the problem of elite corruption and consumer intensive lifestyles that waste resources vital to the survival of the poor and preclude the healthier development of the country as a whole. Since the abrupt loss of cheap oil supplies in the mid-1970s was widely blamed for the deepening economic crisis on a global scale, and made the West suddenly insecure about the Third World as suppliers of critical resources, this experience with oil encouraged a scramble for other 'strategic' resources. Stockpiling by some powers of these resources has created artificial scarcities; these tendencies force prices up and further harm many less developed countries that are required to import such commodities.

The autonomy of the already vulnerable Third World States is also further eroded by the tendency of international funding agencies operating beneath the banner of allegedly sounder criteria of financial management; transnational corporations intensify the economic pressure by cornering natural resources and often distorting capital and production uses. Often the ruling elites of these countries blame international factors, while they themselves diminish the autonomy of local communities by the use of State economic organs to penetrate community economies and by building up inefficient public sectors. The extraction of resources by the State has contributed to hunger, destitution, distress-migration, growing urban rural disparities and cultural destruction on an alarming scale. These interactions have contributed to the rise of social violence in a variety of forms which, in turn, sets in motion tendencies that produce State repression which is justified in the name of maintaining 'law and order'.

The countervailing forces working to overcome the economic crisis are as yet weak. Peace movements have not been able so far to reverse the trends towards rising military expenditures. Renewed labour militancy in advanced industrial countries—for instance, the miners in Britain or Solidarity in Poland—has not, as yet, reversed governmental priorities. The demand for a NIEO by the developing countries has been stymied. Attempts at the assertion of control over natural resources by some Third World countries have failed or have been further weakened by economic factors of over-supply relative to the market. The OPEC phenomenon was for a while, indeed, a success story (but subsequently coopted by the prevailing global economic and military power systems) but other attempts at cartel-building for copper, rubber, coffee and bauxite among others have been frustrated by factors specific to a given commodity and by the deliberate efforts of developed countries. The socialist States have been generally able to withstand the impact of the global economic crisis somewhat better than the market economies of the Third World. However, signs of weakness and of distortions under the impact of consumerism, spread through the mass media and tourism, is apparent in some socialist countries. The kind of de-linking from the world economy that the socialist States were able to achieve through the mid-1970s is not realisable in the case of most Third World States for a whole variety of reasons; some are historical and others are a reflection of the current interplay of political forces.

Militarisation and the global economic crisis have together made the existing conflicts over natural resources more acute and created additional conflicts over newly identified 'strategic' resources. At the global level, conflicts over areas containing resources such as the continental shelves, the sea-bed, Antarctica, and even space, have been growing more intense. In fact, a new category of conflicts over non-material resources such as radio-frequencies and satellite parking orbits has been emerging. Severe concerns about such man-made 'dis-resources' as nuclear waste and pollution of the land, waters and the atmosphere are growing evident in many places. These concerns are likely to become even more acute as modern technology continues to despoil nature on an increasing scale without taking adequate precautions including environmental protection measures and adequate conservation programmes. Resource-related international conflicts contribute to militarisation specifically oriented to the protection of 'national interests'.

Domestically, misguided 'development' policies, pursued by many ruling elites of the Third World, have led to deforestation and desertification on a massive scale. Lands belonging to tribal communities have been heedlessly taken over for mining and industrial purposes. As a result the survival of the distinct cultures of many ancient communities—and in some cases their very physical survival—has become alarmingly precarious. In the developed countries the consequences of man-made dis-resources are growing more severe all the time. And, alienation and anomie arising out of mass-production and consumerism is taking its toll particularly in the form of generalised urban unrest, growth of crime, vandalism, mental illness, drug and alcohol dependencies, and breakdown of family structures. Considered as global trends both cultural and physical survival are threatened.

Once again, a large number of popular movements are the most encouraging countervailing forces rising to stem the tide of misuse and wastage of natural resources and battling to protect the environment against man-made dis-resources. Many of these movements are fighting only on the local scene, often acting in isolation. But their quest is generally similar; it is a search for alternative human technologies, equity in access to resources, simpler life-styles, respect for nature and cultural autonomy, protecting victims, and trying to make sure that those interests responsible for harm are held accountable. There are a variety of efforts underway to overcome the isolation and fragmentation of these initiatives, to build links and networks, and to launch 'macro' initiatives to deal with the deeper causes of local crises, as well as to enhance leverage on the centres of political and economic power.

Our matrix should be seen as basically an heuristic device, a way of checking out that we have considered the implications of each dimension. Of course, the number of dimensions is somewhat selective; further dimensions could be added. Initially, we envisaged a political dimension and a technological dimension. But as we investigated the interlinkages, a set of common themes in each story began to emerge, a set that could provide the basis for telling a new story of global consequence. The role of the State, the shift from liberator to oppressor and from consent to coercion, and the rigidity of existing State priorities was one theme in this new story. The attitude to technology, the belief in a materialist technological fix, based on particular modes of science that claim universalism, was another. These themes did not, however, seem amenable to treatment as the fifth and sixth dimensions. They helped instead to explain the failure of past solutions or alternatives to the crisis, and they offered a new approach which could be adopted as a guide to future social action.

Failed Alternatives

The history of the post-war world is also a history of largely unsuccessful attempts to slow down the arms race, to alleviate poverty in the Third World, or to uphold the rights of oppressed peoples. Despite several decades of efforts, starting with the Baruch Plan in 1946, the comprehensive proposals for disarmament in the 1950s and early 1960s followed by the real but limited arms control agreements of the 1960s and 1970s such as the Partial Test Ban Treaty or the Biological Weapons Convention, it is possible to conclude,

Conclusion: Transforming the State

as Alva Myrdal has argued and documented in the *Game of Document* that no real disarmament was achieved and hardly any tangible results of the immense arms control efforts. Similarly the world economic crisis and the economic crisis in different countries have been the focus of attention of eminent economists all over the world. Alternating theories of rapid industrialisation and green revolution, of import substitution or export-led growth, of floating exchange rates or complex tariff structures, of Keynesianism versus monetarism, have all been applied at different times or at different places. And yet the vast majority of the world's population remains desperately poor. Violation of human rights and the problems of cultural survival have also been frequently considered by organs of the United Nations and have received concerted attention from Amnesty International, the International Law Commission, a variety of voluntary organisations dedicated to upholding human rights, including the rights of women and children in developed and developing countries, as well as those of ethnic and religious minorities. And yet despite all of this there is no alleviation of human oppression. To be sure some notable specific achievements here and there have occurred. But that is all.

Most of these attempts at solutions have been unidimensional and fragmented in the face of multidimensional and synergistic challenges. The multidimensional malaise from which the world is suffering is based on the very same assumptions that underline attempted solutions. The assumptions which underlay the dominant post-1945 paradigms of 'security' and 'development' have been widely criticised; if anything, the criticisms have been continuous and have contributed to thinking about alternatives, but, in general, such criticisms have not questioned the underlying assumptions.

Among the first to question the 'security' paradigm in a serious way were scientists. The Russell-Einstein manifesto of 1955 was followed by the establishment of the Pugwash movement and the emergence of the first 'Ban the Bomb' movements in Europe during the late 1950s. Their concern was with the frailty of national sovereignty in a nuclear age, and the corresponding need for global cooperation and for a common sense of humanity. Their efforts helped precipitate the arms control agreements of the 1960s especially the Partial Test Ban Treaty, but they did not generate any wider transformative process.

The advent of détente, partly as a result of these efforts, and the improved relationship between the East and the West that characterised the 1960s and early 1970s brought forth a new critique of the security paradigm. The fact that the arms race continued despite arms control agreements and détente, focussed attention on the domestic causes of the arms race. In the United States, a rich literature on the military-industrial complex and on bureaucratic politics began to emerge, while in Europe, a new breed of peace researchers worked up structuralist or configurative analyses of the arms race that called attention persuasively to some underlying and neglected factors.

Alongside this new intellectual focus was a growing interest in issues of disarmament and development. It arose initially out of the experience of the Vietnam war and from an increasing realisation that the East-West issues obscured the dynamics of North-South military relations. A series of UN reports detailed the diversion of resources away from development, a diversion constantly abetted by the arms race, especially by the growing military R&D. In addition, a number of scholars began to examine the way in which the network of military aid and intervention, arms trade and production, served to uphold inequitable power structures which were inimical to 'development'.

These concerns were followed in the late 1970s and early 1980s with a renewed interest in European security problems following the signing of the Helsinki Act in 1975. To the questioning of the concepts of 'balance' and 'parity', which had begun with the scientists in the 1950s, was added a questioning of the alliance system in Europe, its connection to the nuclear arms race and the underlying question of the growing perceived use of nuclear war. This ferment has given rise to proposals for nuclear free zones, for the removal of certain types of weapons from Central Europe including Cruise and Pershing II missiles and short-range battlefield nuclear weapons, as well as to ideas about alternative non-provocative defence policies and the gradual withdrawal, or at least a thinning out, of the superpower military presence in both halves of Europe.

Conclusion: Transforming the State

Increasingly sophisticated critiques of the 'security' paradigm began at the very moment, in the 1950s, when the bipolar system was established. Likewise, the first major critique of the 'development' paradigm took place very soon after the model began to be widely accepted by governing elites round the world. This critique became known as 'dependency theory', elaborated by a series of Latin American intellectuals who persuasively insisted that the underdevelopment of Third World societies was an essential aspect of the continuing development of the 'developed' societies. The contributions of this school are by now well-known although there are many subtle variations in approach and conceptual detail. Dependency thinkers focussed on the principal themes of dominance and dependence in the Western hemisphere and highlighted the global context of national and local patterns of development and underdevelopment, putting emphasis on the impacts of the multinational corporations' financial activity in various sectors of the economy.

The next major source of dissent from development theory came from ecological schools that developed during the late 1960s and attracted considerable global attention after the publication of the Club of Rome Report on the limits of growth in 1972. This perspective was, in turn, criticised by the Bariloche and Sussex groups (as well as by economists and social scientists in India and elsewhere) on the basis of a new criterion of development that moved away from the aggregate notion of growth and towards more distributive ideas associated with the satisfaction of basic needs of all human beings in the locale (nation, region, world) under study. The sense that production could deal with all human needs if properly organised was also in keeping with most Marxist orientations towards development policy. Considerable attention was drawn by the 1972 Stockholm Conference on the Human Environment and Development to environmental issues.

Yet another major threshold in the theory of development was marked by the rise of the self-reliance school of development which was articulated both by certain dissident Western (especially Scandinavian) scholars and some leading Third World thinkers who had begun to express serious misgivings about entering the world market and were sensitive to the global structure of capitalist development. These thinkers were greatly attracted by major experiments in 'de-linking', most notably that of China in the first two decades after its revolution. De-linking in various forms implies basic rejection of a homogeneous, interdependent view of the world and posits a need for new nations to carve out their own distinctive models of development aimed at achieving a self-reliant path of progress principally based on the mobilisation of their own resources and their own capabilities. The decade of the 1970s saw the emergence and crystallisation of this way of thinking.

Concurrently with the basic needs and self-reliance schools, there arose a more militant and cohesive Third World critique, mounted by certain articulate spokespersons within the Group of 77 in the U.N. This perspective received great attention, especially as it was followed by the successful, if temporary, challenge to Western hegemony mounted by OPEC in the 1970s. This momentum achieved adoption of the Charter of The New International Economic Order in 1974 despite the misgivings of many developed countries, especially the United States. This demand for a new international economic order remains a major force in the thinking on development in various parts of the Third World and among some dissident scholars in the Western countries, despite a period of discouragement that has included unabashed resistance from the North.

Many, if not all, of these strands of thinking were included in the concept of 'another development', 'alternative development strategies', 'common security', a 'paradigm shift' towards the various alternatives, and so forth. These intentions slowly began to be reflected in official and semi-official circles. A series of United Nations sponsored conferences on such vital issues of human and planetary concern as environment, population, food and human settlements, under the auspices of the non-aligned movement, the UN Special Sessions on Disarmament in 1978 and 1982, the emergence of the Group of 77 and the initiatives of a few heads of State, the series of UN sponsored semi-official seminars and workshops that sparked off the 'Development Decade' and, on top of all this, new expressions of global concern through the establishment and reports of independent commissions (the Brandt Commission and

Conclusion: Transforming the State

the Palme Commission on Disarmament and Security being the most publicised among these but also the McBride Commission on the new information order and the more recently formed Independent Commission on International Humanitarian Issues) have all been expressions of these reforming inclinations.

Each of these responses has enlisted the support of leading world figures and a great deal of industry and effort, each has made an effort to provide new conceptions and a string of practical recommendations, and each has had some impact on world public opinion including on arguably the most influential of all institutions composing the 'Establishment'—the mass media. And yet nothing seems to be changing: governments and corporations and scientists seem to be as busy as ever pursuing their oppressive and destructive ends of power and profits, thereby disempowering human enterprise and endangering the quality and even the possibility, of the future. These forces of the *status quo* have also put roadblocks in the way of reformist thinking at every stage, devoting their vast resources to a massive effort to discredit and sidetrack Third World grievances and to divest well-meaning demands for a serious arms control effort.

Why is this enormous investment of human energy and resources by some of the world's more energetic and creative individuals unable to redirect and restructure the world and is instead producing a rising sense of frustration and despair? A full answer to this question calls for detailed probes into the structure of power and interest that dominates much of the world and even into the deeper recesses of the contemporary human mind. While it is not possible to conduct such explorations here we may mention some of the factors. The first, which has been stressed throughout this volume, is the tendency to adopt unidimensional approaches to multidimensional problems. Although many of the critiques do deal with interlinkages, e.g. disarmament and development or environment and development, they have not produced holistic analyses of the overall disorder that has gained any substantial following. The consequence is often a strange mixture of limited vision and utopian formula in which the investigation of one dimension produces a proposal that does not take into account the consequences and resistances from other dimensions. These proposals neither impress the powers that be nor do they inspire movements for transformation. In the last analysis, such policy advocacy can be, and are, safely disregarded by both sides in the power equation.

But there are two other reasons, perhaps more basic, that explain the paralysis. Such difficulties apply as much to the alternative intellectual models that have emerged over time as to the more action-oriented conferences and commissions. First, most of the thinking so far on alternatives has been by and large addressed to the State and the international order. Further, it has been based on the assumption that the political process takes place in arenas governed by rationality, persuasion and good faith. We should have realised all along that larger and darker forces are at work, that significant advances in the human condition more often result from struggle than persuasion, that even basic changes in the outlook of governments cannot themselves take us much closer to an alternative world. To get anywhere on the plane of action we will have to produce a more adequate account of the whole process of power and distribution beyond relations between States. In essence, our conceptualisation will have to visualise the essential political process as primarily dependent on relations between peoples. And by so doing, we will be led to discover and identify more promising agents of change and catalysts of transformation, mobilisation and renewal.

Second, and in some ways the most basic consideration of all, is the fact that most of these efforts, both theoretical and substantive, exhibit an essentially apolitical approach to development. Developmental issues have been treated as abstract scientific problems for which solutions can be found without any reference to influences exerted over time by historical or political context. No doubt, a part of the debate has been motivated by political considerations, as for example, that part of self-reliance and NIEO schools that aim at building sufficient individual and collective power for States in the Third World. But these attempts share a conception of development as bundles of goods and services proceeding through a trickledown approach in some formulations and through an egalitarian approach in others, premised upon either a growth orientation or a 'basic needs' orientation. Little systematic thought has been given to the

Conclusion: Transforming the State

importance of the model of structural properties that would shift the focus from welfarism of elites to control over the development process by the people; such thought must be based on the deepening of democracy, as well as on a conception of a just and participant society. Even the basic Latin American critique, while emphasising important international dimensions, generally tends to focus on economic and technological factors and concomitant structures of exploitation and dependence between and within societies.

Likewise, arms control and disarmament proposals have failed to take into account the power structures within which armament decisions are taken. It has been frequently observed that those in power lack the will to disarm. But who is in power? The politicians, the arms manufacturers, the armed forces? Though often prompted by a basically political concern, the analysis of historical processes often failed to relate itself to the specific nature of regimes, forms of participation and a clear view on the political prerequisites of achieving desirable forms of peace and socio-economic transformation.

And yet, during the same period (the sixties and the seventies), there has also emerged from a few thinkers a more comprehensive critique of disarmament and development thinking. The thinkers, while drawing upon the dependency, ecological, basic needs, self-reliance and NIEO streams in a more holistic framework, has focussed on the need to deal with poverty, inequity and oppression as essentially interrelated political and cultural tasks. This larger critique has not taken the form of a very specialised school like the other mentioned above. It has emerged from a variety of vantage points and is, of late, receiving attention by theoreticians, movements of dissent and even policy analysts in different parts of the world.

It is within this genre of new thinking on development, often *against* 'development' or 'security' as laid out in the traditional doctrines of development and security, that our attempt in the programme on Peace and Global Transformation of the United Nations University and its integral view of development, peace and freedom belongs. Only in the last few years has the realisation dawned on thinkers of development that, in their preoccupation with socio-economic issues, the traditional concern with human freedom has oddly been left out.

Our Vision

We call our vision of a preferred future 'a liberating peace'. Our presentation of the multi-dimensional disorder is necessarily informed by a holistic vision. This vision provides the touchstone for defining immediate and intermediate goals. Fundamental to our vision are changed assumptions about human beings and nature, transformation of the concept of power and an insistence that means must be treated as part of ends.

Our vision takes peace as a condition of life itself. It is a life-sustaining peace, sustaining nature and its resources, sustaining values that protect and nurture coherence and inter-relatedness, that promote a just social order through a democratic process that is based on the freedom of each as the condition of freedom of all. It is a stable peace, not just a cease-fire. This implies a culture of non-violence which is widely accepted, but in a militant spirit of dedication to the goals of societal self-control and restraint in the ordering of human needs, passions and ambitions.

The real test of such a liberating peace is that the global peripheries and the poor and the oppressed acquire a vital stake in its attainment. The concept of the nation-State loses its centrality and potency; global and local institutions and processes acquire far more importance. These interact on the basis of non-violent political action at all levels. A participatory politics incorporating discussion, debate, negotiation and compromise, mediation; it is a politics that responds to people's demands including especially valuing those of the currently marginal and disenfranchised minorities.

In societies that embody our visions, standards of happiness would be based primarily on human relationships and individual actualisation, not on material possessions and conspicuous consumption. The models of development adopted by such a societal disposition would necessarily, without any special added effort, also be models of peace; modes of 'development' which constitute threats to peace would be rejected in favour of what has been called voluntary simplicity, even in instances verging on shared austerity. These

Conclusion: Transforming the State

societies would refuse to borrow against the resource capital of the planet at the expense of future generations. It would be development that relies on consensus about the nature of the human enterprise and its balance with nature, and one that affirms in practical ways the basic unity of humanity while simultaneously valuing the diversity that enriches and strengthens the species. All this would arise quite naturally from a suitably integrated epistemology of transformation, displacing current approaches that are highly specialised and disjointed.

Science in such a world would have the primary role of satisfying human curiosity and contributing to the ecologically sound satisfaction of human needs, including those associated with the non-material aspects of fulfilment. It would be only *one* knowledge-system among many and with no special claims to achieve universal truth, any more than would alternate modes of knowledge and wisdom. In fact, we conceive of a plurality of sciences, each with its own interpretation of the objective reality but tolerant of and learning from other interpretations to enrich itself. Technology would apply scientific understanding of various kinds to alleviate degrading labour, enhancing human potential, avoiding the exploitation of animals and the deterioration of nature. It would be a series of technologies that represent and collaborate with nature instead of trying to conquer it. Acceptance of plurality in the realm of science and technology would be a further expression of an affirming attitude towards cultural diversity, religious, ideological and political plurality and the personal dignity of males, females, children, old people as well as those suffering from disabilities or choosing deviant patterns of life style not harmful to others. A broad ethos of tolerance is implied in our vision.

We have, frankly, come dangerously close to presenting one more utopian vision. Many utopias of this type have been offered to a bleeding humanity in the past. We are aware of them and the failure they have been. We have also studied the historical lessons from brutalising attempts to impose utopias on society. Utopias generate their own pathologies that cannot be altogether anticipated in advance. Ours is a somewhat different effort. We have tried to provide a vision and a perspective, not a blue-print for massive, purposive human engineering, and *not* a dogmatic insistence that there is a single right way to do things or to enter the promised land. In fact, we believe that neither blue-prints nor dogmas can bring a liberating peace.

Our vision comprises a series of quite general goals that we propose as 'generating themes' to help orient the work and dreams of movements and campaigns. Such goals are already inspiring people in different historical, geographical and cultural situations to undertake action and engage in non-violent struggle in the light of the concrete conditions in which they find themselves.

Immediate and intermediate goals have already been frequently identified by new forces and actors working for peace and transformation. These goals include peace and conflict resolution between States, nuclear and conventional disarmament, promotion of civil liberties and democratic rights, protection of cultural autonomy, an improved gender balance, economic delinking and self-reliance at various levels within and among States, an economic order based on community-based and eco-oriented development, a less materialistic culture, political decentralisation and responsive political institutions at all societal levels, a humane science and technology working for the people as a whole and subject to popular control and priorities. The list of goals is long and will grow as more and more people, groups and countries introduce new emphases in responpse to the specific impact of oppressive circumstance on concrete conditions and on the consciousness of victims and their movements.

The intellectual challenge to the research communities of the United Nations University and to the intellegentsia as a whole is to establish more credible connections among the intermediate goals. This will permit more holistic responses to the various challenges. The synergy of the specific processes towards attaining goals will unleash transformative power far beyond a given set of circumstances. Such synergy means that an intermediate goal in the economic realm—or along any other dimension—should be conceived so that its transformative effects are experienced, to the largest extent possible, in other realms. By the same token, action on any of the spatial levels,—global, regional or national—should be conceived and enacted so that it would exert influence at other levels. To

Conclusion: Transforming the State

borrow an analogy from acupuncture (or any system of holistic medicine) the needling of a point on the ear is intended to affect the heart, perhaps also the kidney, but not necessarily the ear itself. Our sense of desirable politics, then, is to induce beneficial rippling processes that suffuse the whole of the body politic, regardless of where particular pressures arise or curative therapies are originated.

Strategies of Transformation

Some States, including certain of the socialist States, are already seeking to transform the existing international State-system in desirable directions. Similarly, new actors—women, youth, organised peasants and tribals, concerned intellectuals, scientists, citizen groups, peace movements, green movements, and grassroot movements for social justice—are struggling to achieve the goals and orientations enumerated above. But their efforts continue to be fragmented to varying degrees and often remain too unidimensional and localised, although an increasing list of encouraging exceptions could be mentioned. We acknowledge, at the same time, that a particular focus in response to a specific danger may be essential, especially if an emergency situation exists.

It seems to us that since it is the State which is the most crucial actor on the international scene as well as being the central embodiment of power—whether political, military, economic, social or even cultural—transformation of the State must become the key to any strategy of transition to a better future. As we have said in the Introduction to this volume, the State was originally conceived, if somewhat unconvincingly, as having a liberating role, a role that the modern State seems to have unwittingly abandoned in many settings. In fact, the State has become a prime source of oppression in many parts of the world. It is imperative that the State once again plays a liberating role, but such a prospect can only be realised through the enabling effects of a new politics from below that can reconstitute the agenda and outlook of State and its official leadership.

Seizure of State-power by a particular class or vanguard of the oppressed is not the solution. All too often in the history of our times, the capture of State power by those with a counter-ideology, whether secular or religious, has merely led to a greater and more efficient concentration of power in the State and its network of institutions. As a result, the successive form of State has become even more oppressive than it was under the former regime. In the liberating State of our vision, politics must remain at all times responsive to the people's demands, including those of minorities and deviant life modes, while these demands themselves be expressed within a framework of values embodying attitudes of tolerance, non-violence, and conservation of all forms of life. Action, whether by the State or by citizens, must be guided by an implicit framework of respect for life and human dignity, without constraints of space or time.

The strategy for transforming the State, then, needs to be based on a programme of reclaiming power for the people, power that has been usurped, not only by the State, but by political parties and governmental procedures as well. This means enhancing the role of voluntary organisations and other non-State actors. It also means encouraging coordinated activity and networks across national borders and in regional arenas. And these non-State actors, so activated, need to organise themselves in new ways, not primarily along party and electoral lines, as has been the case in the past—a story of growing failure—but as groups that continuously, on a day-to-day basis imbibe the historical experience of a particular society, its political culture, the nature of issues and whatever other factors seem to embody the broad holistic outlook.

In a sense, the research agenda for our programme in the UN University to describe what State transformation means in institutional terms. How can power be spread among different State institutions, i.e., global, national, regional or local? What are the responsibilities of, say, the OAU or the EEC as compared with those of the United Nations, Germany or Nigeria, or with the local governments of Stuttgart or Lagos? How can power be spread among the institutions of the State, e.g., ministries, parliament, political parties? How can power be shifted and dispensed globally, away from bipolar and multipolar concepts that have prevailed so far in the post-war era? And above all, how can the State and its agents be held accountable by those social movements most capable

Conclusion: Transforming the State

of acting as agents of transformation and as representatives of popular will? Those responsible for environmental or political abuses are at least as 'criminal' as those who commit assaults on city streets.

Agents of Transformation

Throughout this volume we have spoken of new forces on the international scene (especially the post-colonial States, but also other States that take positive initiatives) and the new actors on the national scene (peace and ecological movements in the North, grass-root movements in the South, movements for democratic rights in the East) in a positive vein. Obviously, we do not endorse all new forces and movements as having a desirable orientation towards working for a liberating peace nor do we condemn Statism unreservedly. After all, the post-colonial State has indeed liberated its citizens from alien domination and is even today often protecting its sovereignty *vis-a-vis* neo-imperialist forces and the transnational corporations. But the ideology of militant nationalism that has been widely adopted as the supreme article of faith provides at the same time, a stimulus for militarisation, anti-people development orientation, centralisation of political power, and interference with cultural autonomy. A liberating peace can never be achieved by a nation-State that puts national security before peoples's security and national interest above people's interests.

Similarly with the new people's movements. We obviously do not endorse movements that are based on religious or other forms of fundamentalism and are intolerant of the diversity of religious beliefs and cultural practices. We regard as regressive the growth of 'movements of the majority' that seek to impose one or another type of homogeneity on the minorities. We do not endorse groups that impose their economic demands on the society, demands that can be met only by sacrificing the welfare of other groups in the society. And we can see no role for movements based on ideologies that make unconditional claims about possessing the truth about nature and society. All such pretensions of certainty are a betrayal of the plural character that pertains to the human situation.

While emphasising the role of people's movements, we also value the role of congenial actors and individuals who find themselves working in State institutions, the UN system and other international organisations but want to see the State and the international system transformed in a similar spirit. Traditionally, international civil servants are apolitical functionaries; over the years they have become more and more politicised. They know the working of the 'Establishment' and can either help people's movements to make the State more responsive to popular demands, or serve out their time as bureaucratic pawns of Statist pressures exerted from behind the scene. Since the object is to transform the State rather than capture or smash it, the cooperation of concerned bureaucrats, scientists, and even policemen and soldiers becomes extremely valuable. We believe it is attainable. They too are often disenchanted with the workings of the State and need popular encouragement to join in as active supporters of the process of transformation.

Our analysis shows that catastrophe could come by means other than by actions of the superpowers or by mad men poised to strike at the soft points of the modern world. Catastrophe could also result from the unchecked interplay of 'normal' forces that now take a tragic human and ecological toll. By the same token, we believe that initiatives for a movement towards a liberating peace need not come from great statesmen and well-trained experts, but from ordinary men and women engaged in the struggle to enhance their destiny.

The global crisis has undoubtedly created a new sense of a common stake in the future of humanity among many ordinary people. But most responses, as we have seen, have heretofore been largely limited to immediate demands and urgencies. And these responses do not build towards the future, but sputnik after an initial spasm of reactive energy. Enterprises for change fall short of expectations and disillusion their adherents. As yet there has been little movement from a fire-fighting mentality to a more unified understanding of the challenge. A common vision shared by movements in the West and the East, in the North and the South has not yet even begun to take hold. There is a set of mortal dangers, but as yet no global response. The knowledge generated by the new forces and the diverse, often fragmented and frequently isolated, movements is waiting to unfold new frameworks of holistic analysis and to evolve new programmes of synergetic action.

Conclusion: Transforming the State

To facilitate grassroot self-discovery processes is, in our view, the overriding and most valuable research challenge of our time. We are aware of our limits as thinkers and researchers and we are deeply conscious of the fact that research is not enough. It is, at best, only a beginning. Knowledge by itself does not generate either wisdom or right action. It is only when various bits of knowledge form part of a holistic process that arises from and corresponds to one's experience of social forces on the field, on which more genuine comprehension and wisdom must be based, can research hope to influence and serve as a catalyst and resource. We are also acutely aware of the limitations of any secular framework of analysis. However complete and inclusive such a framework claims or seeks to be, its acceptability among people diversely situated will always remain low. It is important not to confuse dogmatic recipes and vague generalities with a holistic research. Any universalist credo unless rooted in the concreteness of struggle leads to discredited reality of unrestrained secularism. We reject the rigid separatism of spiritual and secular, and call for a creative fusion of the two, endowing a here-and-now search with an appreciation of the sacred quality of life and, more generally, of transcendental values. The vision of a liberating peace, we believe, is inspiring and elevating because it summons the spiritual energies of peoples and because this vision of the desirable is not permanently beyond human reach. The utopian element in it, to the extent it exists, is not a consequence of setting goals beyond societal capacities, but the assumption that constructive forces can gain the upper hand in the historical process. This evocation of human potential is a plea for a new elan, in effect a call. The call of a liberating peace.